Prema Agni
Symbol as described in the book.

STOP THE STRUGGLE

LIVE FULLY, BE HAPPY

Derek O'Neill

Front Cover Design: © 2020 by Derek O'Neill
Cover photographs by Dreamstime and Unsplash

For information about permission to reproduce excerpts from this book write to:
Derek O'Neill
244 5th Avenue, Suite D-264
New York, NY 10001
E-Mail: info@derekoneill.com | www.derekoneill.com

You may order this book directly from the author's website.

ISBN: 978-1-936470-76-1

Stop The Struggle Is A Memoir of Teaching, Learning and Self-Understanding That Will Change Your Life

(If You Let It)

TABLE OF CONTENTS

CHAPTER 1

The Pain That Molds Us

"It is essential for you to encourage the positive emotions as dominating forces of your mind, and to discourage – and eliminate – negative emotions." Napoleon Hill

Lesson: Finding Your Emotional Pivot Points

My mother seemingly resented me. And it wasn't my fault. I was an innocent fetus in the womb when events happened that changed the emotional climate of our home.

It was when my pregnant mother returned home early from work one day to the sound of desperate rustling upstairs in their bedroom. At first, she may have thought it was a burglar, but some instinct drove her up the stairs anyway. She opened the door to their bedroom and found her husband and her best friend scrambling to put on their clothes. Desperate apologies were made, tears of anger were shed, promises made. I heard all about it over the years from my siblings. I also heard that from that day on, my mother was never the same.

Within days she began drinking alcohol, all day, every day. This came as a shock to my brothers and sisters. They said she drank very little before catching our father with another woman. But now heavy drinking became her main interest. It was as though she wanted to drink her problems away. Looking back, I think my mother wanted to be free of my father and she saw another baby as holding her in an unwanted marriage. I believe she not only wanted to drink me to death, but also herself. She was in severe pain and wanted it to end.

From that day forward my parents never slept in the same bedroom again. Our house was a silent war zone. My deceived mother acted almost as though her husband was dead. And my father became an angry man, blowing up at the most unexpected of times.

My older brothers and sisters defined life around the house as being "before the event" and "after the event." "Before the event," all was normal, said one of my older brothers. Life was light and mom and dad were happy with their children and with each other. "After the event," the family became a study in dysfunction. It was as though a sort of Dark Ages of emotional intelligence settled on the O'Neill household.

You can pretty much guess what happened after that. When formidable people in our lives don't give us enough attention, the struggle begins. We no longer believe that we are worthy of their love or understanding, and we feel a void that needs to be filled. And we fill it. Sometimes anger does the trick, or drugs and alcohol, or food, or promiscuity, or hate. That's almost always the way it works.

I feel confident in saying that if you don't have a void that needs to be filled, then someone close to you has one. And I will go even further in saying that these voids are the result of pivot points, powerful events involving formidable people that can determine how we see ourselves and how we react to the world around us. Pivot points can be either demoralizing or moralizing; as when you meet a person of authority in your childhood who makes you feel good about yourself and gives you confidence that lasts a lifetime. As I have learned, there is goodness and grace all around us; we need only develop the ability to experience it.

But the sad fact is that negative events in a person's life carry far more emotional weight than the positive. I am not sure why this is true, but I do notice in both my patients, and the general public, that people focus far more on negative events than positive. And those negative events – even seemingly small ones – carry a much greater ability to damage a person, than larger positive events do to heal them.

That said, the pivot points that came from my parents were consistently negative. I won't violate the confidentiality of my siblings by dealing with their pivot points. And I won't tell you all of mine because it would take up too many pages. But I will say that three of the four oldest siblings had wonderful years growing up. My oldest brother, John, was the apple of my parents' eyes, as many oldest children are. The second oldest was Brian, whose sad life will be covered in a later chapter. And then there was Jean, who has two children. The same is true of Mary, who looks at me with bemusement when I talk about the horrors of my childhood. They were the first four children and were several years older and quite distant from the batch I came from, that included an older brother Des and a younger one, Paul.

The younger three of us were the ones who suffered from the war between our parents. "Civilian casualties," was how my younger brother described us. He was right. We suffered the brunt of the war. Whether they were engaged in outright battle or psychological warfare with one another, there was always some kind of spillover of bad emotions onto us, events that were damaging pivot points that we all remember to this day. In our own way, and using the belief systems we individually built up, i.e. many different versions of the same story, that does not matter as we all have to choose to deal or not. An example would be us sitting at the dinner table with my mother saying, "Ask your father to pass the salt", and my father answering, "Tell your mother she has arms still".

It was not easy to watch my mother dislike herself. She expressed her resentment of me at every opportunity it seemed, revealing it in her facial expressions every time she looked at me, and in her voice when she spoke to me. Yet there was a secret of how much she really loved me underneath this. And I was to find out later that this was a kind of test to see if I would abandon her as well. When I was around my mother I struggled with feelings of self-worth. Around her I was always a bad person who reminded her of her husband's transgressions, which was painful since I loved my mother dearly.

4

My earliest memories are of my mother yelling at me and slapping me. Her violence became worse as I aged, and, at a very early age, it reached a more violent turning point. I was walking through the kitchen as she was doing dishes, and for some unexplained reason I picked up her bottle of vodka and moved it to the living room. I don't remember why I did this, but when I came back through the kitchen on my way out of the house, she was working herself into a rage because she was unable to find her precious drink.

"I moved it to the living room," I said nervously.

With no warning she took the plate she was holding and whacked me on the head. The room went black for a moment as pieces of the plate showered to the ground.

Being hit by the plate didn't hurt that much, but my heart was broken. I looked at mom and had no sense that she felt an act of abuse or humiliation had taken place. She looked at me for a moment with dead eyes, and when I didn't move she went back to washing dishes.

"Don't do that again," she said. "Leave my things alone."

I left the house holding my head, but I should have been holding my heart. My sense of self-worth plummeted, although – surprisingly – my desire to make my mother love me rose. I even went so far as to go into the woods near our home and pick her a bouquet of wildflowers.

This desire to make her love me culminated in deep fear that I was going to lose her. And it was that fear that led to experiences of extreme empathy, even seemingly psychic moments, that drove us further apart. I was aware she was drinking herself to death.

One Saturday morning, for example, I was watching cartoons on television when I envisioned my mother being killed in a bus crash. The vision took only seconds, but it showed me in vivid images – the bus hurtling down the hill, ending up on its side, with my mother and the other passengers being thrown through the windows and being horribly cut. The vision was relevant to that night because every Saturday my mother took a bus down Christ Church Hill into Dublin City Center to join her friends for drinks. These Saturday nights were important to mom because she said, "That is where my real family is."

It was a horrible vision and one I could not overcome. I kept seeing the bus rolling over, like the driver had lost his brakes and could do nothing to slow down and navigate a sharp curve. I spent the day plotting to keep her off the 6:50 bus to city center. I had to save her life.

I concocted a plan. Late in the afternoon I began complaining about cramps. I told her I felt sick and that she needed to stay home and care for me. That approach didn't work at all. She was already drunk – in preparation for that evening when she would get even drunker – and her only advice to me was to go outside and play.

As the day wore on, I realized that pretending to be ill wouldn't be enough. I changed my tact completely. I watched the clock and listened to mom as she put on her makeup and did her hair. When I heard the hiss of hairspray, which was the signal that she was almost ready to leave, I ran up the stairs and stormed into her bedroom.

"I'm sick and tired of having nobody in this house who cares about me," I shouted. "I'm going to kill myself."

I ran into the bathroom, opened my father's Wilkinson's Sword razor, pretending I was going to slit my wrists. Locking the bathroom door behind me, after they saw me, I sat on the floor with my back behind the door and my feet against the toilet bowl, and a big fuss broke out. Finally, the door was pushed open and I was dragged out. My mother's hand was first in the room, its open palm smacking hard against my cheek. Mission successful, she had missed the bus, I had kept her home. What was a sharp slap in exchange for saving the life of my mother?

Psychic moment or not, there was a bus crash that night I was told. The 6:50 bus was going down Christ Church Hill when it was hit by another vehicle and pushed off the road. Several passengers were injured and when my mother heard about the accident, she never spoke about it. I felt a psychic moment had saved my mother. I also believed that the vision I had was caused by the amount of love I had for her. I still believe that.

This vision became a stabilizing block for me in the years ahead. The idea of seeing an accident before it happened, and saving a loved one as a result, connected me with a higher power. I realized that pure love was a conduit to a sixth sense. It would be years later before I would be given the techniques to access that sixth sense at will. Briefly, these techniques include mindfulness, meditation, walking and being in nature with the plants, trees and animals. These forms of meditation use nature's five elements to balance our energy – earth, wind, fire, water and ether. But as a young man desperate for love and attention, it gave me great hope to have firsthand awareness of a higher power.

This vision also allowed me to understand that my mother had lost her connection with a higher power. She no longer had hope. My father's unforgivable act of infidelity was a sort of fatal pivot point for her. His act had changed her so much that she had lost touch with all that was good in her life. She retreated into her internal world making us all feel abandoned. She should have tried to make amends with my father, or had the courage to leave him (an act that would have taken true courage in Catholic Ireland in the 1960s). Instead she became an alcoholic and drank, and drank, and drank, so much that she sometimes forgot why she drank. Perhaps that was the point.

My father, however, never forgot why she drank. Although he never spoke about his act of infidelity it was clearly on his mind at all times. And that led to numerous negative pivot points taking place between us over the years.

Dad's negative pivot points usually involved powerful expressions of anger that came at unexplained times, not at everyone, but, definitely, at me. For example, we were affixing an appliance to the kitchen counter when he dropped a screw on the floor. As he scanned the floor for it my arms tired and the appliance shifted. By the time he found the screw, the holes to the countertop were no longer lined up. All Dad would have had to do was line up the holes and put in the screws. But anger overwhelmed him and instead his response was to rip the appliance from the counter and smash it on the floor.

"Damn you!" he shouted as I ran for cover.

That moment is, unfortunately, the strongest image I have of my father.

As you can see, the most powerful people in my life – my parents – provided some of the most negative and damaging pivot points in my life. That may be the same for you. It may even be far worse than what happened to me. When I talk to patients about negative pivot points, and tell them about my own, they oftentimes list negative pivot points that make mine sound like a good day at play school. Patients will tell me about being beaten bloody by their fathers, or having their mothers abuse them over the most meaningless things. I've even had patients who were locked in closets by their parents for forgetting to take out the trash. One of my patients was locked in a trunk by her father for reasons so meaningless I can't even remember, but I remember my reaction to hearing it.

Sharing these negative pivot points will often result in anger and bitterness, as patients recount incidents that have led them to seek therapy. Sometimes these negative events have happened decades earlier, yet when patients recall them, they flush with anger or break out in tears. Some even become fearful. It's as though the event took place yesterday and they are afraid to go home for fear that this powerful person will be waiting for them. This does not surprise me. Remember, it is these negative pivot points that have led them to lose their sense of self-worth. It is also these negative pivot points that lead them to express the same behavior with those around them. "The sins of the father are visited upon the sons," is an old saying that is true of both genders. Because negative pivot points represent our strongest memories of the formidable people in our lives; they remain close to the surface and are often the first reflex to emerge at times of stress.

A patient I treated, for example, was a very gentle soul except when it came to dealing with her children. When she spoke to them, she usually did it in a rage, sometimes getting physically aggressive. After several hypnotherapy sessions she uncovered memories of her father, who rarely listened to her unless she demanded it in a loud voice. Sometimes she became so demanding of his attention that he would slap her. The odd thing was that she enjoyed the attention.

"Better to be slapped and listened to, than not be listened to at all," she said.

Now as a parent, she found herself doing the same thing her father had done to her. This behavior became her reference point, her negative pivot point.

Negative pivot points are not just reflexive actions, but behaviors we exhibit on a day-to-day basis until they become part of our personalities. So, an angry father begets an angry son, a resentful mother begets a resentful daughter. And so on. No matter what causes these negative pivot points, the result is almost always one or more of such traits as: anger, fear, addiction, shame, or the desire for status, money, love, or acceptance. When these traits become toxic, they contain a void that absorbs a person's life force. They become your own negative pivot points that can affect your work life, your relationships, and even future generations. That's how powerful these negative pivot points are. A positive pivot point is one in which an act of kindness is directed to you.

When my patients understand the concept of negative pivot points, they usually want to talk about them.

Generally, this is a good idea. Talking is one of the great forms of spiritual and emotional release because it brings issues into the light where they can be examined and made less toxic. But there is also a downside to talking about issues, especially negative ones. Over talking negative pivot points can allow them to be rationalized away, or even make them worse. The reality is, what you focus on you manifest more of.

There are people who talk and talk about their negative pivot points but never seem to do anything about them. Sometimes, they speak almost joyfully about the negative pivot points in their lives. It's as though these negative pivot points are seen as important aspects of their identity and not behaviors to overcome. They forget that once they are aware of their negative pivot points, they own them and need to not pass them onto others, but use them to break through to a higher power.

For example, a patient of mine was constantly talking to me about personal empowerment and how she empowered herself by traveling to India. It seemed as though she went to India 10 times a year to attend workshops about personal power and other events. Yet despite her extensive knowledge about personal empowerment, she was financially broke because of the amount of money she gave to her adult children. They did not want to work, and worse, she didn't want them to work. Their wealthy father (her ex-husband) had never treated them very well. Since her desire was to be the "good parent" in the family, she supported them in style, keeping herself in a state of poverty.

Oddly enough she was truly happy in her misery. It made her a martyr, since not only was she suffering for her children, she was able to show suffering to her ex-husband, something she actually thought he cared about.

This became the script of her life, constant complaints about her "money-sucking" children and her "worthless" ex-husband. She knew more about personal empowerment than most of my colleagues, yet she wanted to be identified as a martyr.

There is a delicate balance between talk that is therapeutic and talk that is, well, just talk. For some, these negative pivot points are almost like scenes from a movie in which the person living them has no control. They tend to forget that the movie they are describing is their movie, where the script can always change, and the ending can be anything they want it to be. For example, Kerry was having difficulty with money, in that she couldn't stop spending it. She and her husband made a very good living working as executives in an insurance company, but the bills she ran up buying clothing were actually driving them into debt. It was common for Kerry to spend several hundred dollars per day buying dresses, new suits, shoes, anything fashionable she could put on her body to look better. She was very attractive and knew it. When I first met with her, she told me that she was attractive, yet couldn't stop buying clothing to "put more icing on the cake."

Her husband had asked her many times to stop buying clothing. "At least take a breather," he asked, "until we catch up with the bills." She promised to do just that but didn't keep her promise. Instead she started hiding the credit card bills and just continued – in her husband's words – with her "psychotic buying spree." Her husband finally threatened divorce and even discussed the possibility with a lawyer. That was when she came to see me.

"I can't stop buying clothes," she said. "And to tell the truth, I'm not sure I want to. Being fashionable is what I'm all about."

I nodded my head. The Chanel suit she was wearing made it clear that clothing was very important to her. But why? After two or three sessions of culling through her childhood, I knew that Kerry's family was a large one and had very little money with which to clothe and feed the children.

As one of the middle children among eight brothers and sisters, standing out in the crowd was very important to her, and with few financial resources, the way Kerry chose to do that was through her intellect. She was very good with numbers and became a standout math whiz and always finished in the first five at countrywide math competitions.

She was very proud of her math achievements, and so were her parents, who took every opportunity they could to tout her skills to friends and strangers alike. But pride turned to shame in one thoughtless moment. Kerry had just won the math competition at her high school and was basking in the glory of this intellectual victory. Her parents were with her as she proudly shook the hands of all who were congratulating her when one of the math teachers appeared.

"Kerry is a young genius," he said to her parents while he shook Kerry's hand. "And it's a good thing she is, because sometimes she can look quite shabby."

To Kerry's horror, her father agreed.

"Yes, she can," he said. "We do the best we can but, yes, it's good that she was born smart."

Kerry couldn't remember her parent's frame of mind, or what was said after those thoughtless comments. She immediately went into a cloud of embarrassment and wanted to hide herself from the teacher, her parents, everybody. From that point on, nothing was the same for Kerry.

"I suddenly realized that being a math whiz would only get me noticed among other math whizzes," she said. "But clothing was a sign to the whole world that I was somebody."

Her need for fine clothing started that day and grew into a larger and larger problem. Whenever she got a raise or a bonus, Kerry spent the extra money on clothing because it gave her relief from the shame she felt about her appearance and provided status that she lacked. Over the years her need had turned into an obsession. She was aware of this obsession and aware of the thoughtless moment in her life that had led to this point. That moment obsessed her, too. When she looked in a mirror, she saw herself as a shabby child and heard that painful conversation between powerful adults in her life. She simply was unable to get that pivotal moment out of her head.

I used hypnotherapy with Kerry for some time, but in the end, she refused to rewrite the script she lived by. Sadly, she gave up her husband for shopping. "I can't cut back because I really don't want to cut back," she told me. "That shabby little girl is with me to stay."

It didn't have to be this way, but Kerry was stuck in the negative parts of her life and had failed to look for positive pivot points, ones that would have allowed her to make friends with that shabby little girl.

That was Kerry's problem. She could not, or would not, look for the positive pivot points in her childhood. She would not admit that her parents were excellent at parenting even though they were poor. And she laughed at the idea that her math intellect played an enormous role in her success. Instead she let that shabby little girl define her life. She chose to let her negative pivot points guide her life.

When the patient has clearly outlined the negative pivot points in their life, I remind them that talk is not cheap, nor is it therapeutic, when used improperly. Then, assuming that the patient is truly ready to move on, I introduce them to their positive pivot points.

Many of you reading this right now might snort sarcastically at the notion that you have anything in your life resembling such things as positive pivot points. As you will recall, a positive pivot point is an act of kindness directed toward you. It can be random and short, like a sincere compliment from a stranger, or intentional and sustained, like a neighbor who loves life and all the people in it.

I am sometimes amazed at the number of patients who say they have no positive pivots in their life. I don't believe this is possible. Kindness happens all the time. But, as I have already said, negative pivot points carry far more weight than the positive ones. They embed themselves deeper, and are recalled far quicker, than positive ones. If a person is emotionally sensitive, or if the negative pivot point is especially horrific (as many are), then they can blot out the light from a positive pivot point, sometimes completely.

I have met patients for whom this is true. Some are tremendously successful in life yet have a deep darkness created by the negative in their life. No matter how much they try to achieve, or love, or gain acceptance, it always turns into a struggle. The negative pivot points won't let their lives be anything else. And because of that, they are incapable of seeing the many positive pivot points that have graced their lives.

Jim was one such patient. He was a very successful businessman who was driven by his feelings toward his father, a deep, dark negative force in his life. Jim felt that his father was only truly happy when he was competitive. Unfortunately, his competitiveness knew no bounds. He was competitive in the workplace as well as at home, telling his children they would never come close to matching his success, and then trying to sabotage their success with harsh criticism.

Despite the mental harassment, Jim struggled to succeed and succeed he did. If his wealth didn't equal his father's, it was close. But along with his growing wealth came a diminished sense of self-worth. No matter how much money he made, or toys he acquired, Jim was increasingly less happy. He came to me out of desperation. He honestly felt that life was not worth living.

Jim's problems were made worse by the notion that he owed everything in his life – the bad and good – to his father. "Without my father I wouldn't be rich," he said. "Yet with him I wouldn't be happy."

I didn't try to get Jim to acknowledge his role in his own life, because it didn't seem as though it was worth it. He had the notion that his father was the alpha and omega in his life, and nothing at this point could dissuade him from that line of thought. Many people are like that. They ascribe their successes and failures to other people and refuse to own them themselves. They have become passive. Instead of having drive in their lives, they are being driven by forces outside of themselves, or their subconscious.

What was happening to Jim is what happens to so many successful adults; his confusing and loveless childhood would take over when he thought of his parents.

Now that his father was nearing the age of 85, Jim felt he may never be able to change his toxic relationship with his father. "I can't sit in my country estate and tell him that his attitude ruined me," said Jim. "But I'm not a happy man and getting worse every day. What should I do?"

Listening to Jim was truly painful, but common. Before parents pass away, children want to confront the emotional issues they may have with them. This may not always be possible. Sometimes aged parents are too ill to discuss painful issues, or perhaps don't even know that an issue exists. Sometimes they themselves don't want the pain of discussing emotionally flammable issues. Still, Jim felt cheated by not being able to discuss these issues with his father.

I could sympathize with this point of view. For a time in my own life I felt there was nothing positive to be found. My mother resented me, and my father seemed to hate everything. The strange thing was, my mother had a heart of gold for other people outside our home. It was then that I made an accidental discovery: There is something positive in every life.

I made that discovery in the streets.

I know, most people cringe when someone says they were "raised in the streets". And there is good reason to cringe, given that there are a lot of bad characters out there. But in our overpopulated Dublin neighborhood, it was different in that, the gravity of the good far outweighed the bad. Much of this had to do with the other mothers. They knew about my father's indiscretion with her best friend and could see that she was now struggling with alcohol as a result. They also knew about our problems with Brian, my elder brother. Instead of turning their backs in her time of need, they covered for her.

Without fully realizing it, I had a neighborhood full of surrogate mothers, women who watched out for me, counseled me, disciplined me, and showed love when I could get none at home.

The woman a couple of streets down, Mrs. Fitzpatrick, was a prime example. She would let us all hang around in her house, and made us pots of tea, cookies, and jam sandwiches. Even when there were no cookies, she freely engaged in conversation, asking how life was or how are things? How's your family? How's your ma? She knew my parents were troubled but never voiced an opinion. "Say hello to your ma," she would say.

Her husband Mick was a sort of surrogate father to me. He was interested in nature and would spend weekends taking my friends and I into the woods where he taught us all to fly cast or to catch wild birds to sell.

Sometimes we would camp overnight in the woods where we built small bonfires and ate the fish we caught, but only after we cleaned them ourselves. In the evening we would go back to the Fitzpatrick house where we made big pots of tea and sandwiches with our dirty hands and then sat on the sofa with our dirty trousers to eat.

These were simple moments in my life, but extremely positive ones. To many who read this book, these will seem like nothing, or perhaps commonplace events in their lives. I bring them up in this book to illustrate how simple positive pivot points can be. These were among the most positive events in my childhood, perhaps because they allowed me to forget the negative for a while – stop the struggle, if you will – and live life like a carefree boy.

There were many other positive pivot points in my life too. And yes, they were even more trivial than the examples above, like teachers who were kind when learning was tough, or the bus driver who would smile when I got onboard. They were small pivot points, yet positive ones nonetheless, because they contributed to my sense of self-worth. They were events that helped me gain self-confidence and build faith in myself.

I am not only trying to point out that life is made of good and bad events. You probably knew that in your heart even before you started reading this book. No, what I am pointing out is simply this: once you are aware of these pivot points, you own them. Once I was aware of the resentment by which I was treated by my mother, I had the primary tool with which to keep from treating loved ones with that same resentment. The same goes for the positive pivot points. By maintaining awareness of the good in my life, I could make sure that it was handed down to my loved ones so it could become a positive pivot point for them too.

When I explained the power of positive pivot points to Jim, he got it immediately. Together we searched his life for the positive. As I explained, positive pivot points don't negate negative pivot points, they just take the edge off of them.

"No one's life is entirely negative, it just feels that way," I told him. "The positive pivot points propel you forward, but negative pivot points are stumbling blocks, which is why they get more attention."

Jim got it, and began the exploration of positive pivot points in his life. At first, he had difficulty, but then it became easier as he opened himself to good, although small things, that happened in his life. Here is a partial list of his positive pivot points. I have included that here so you can see how small, yet significant, many of these positive pivot points can be:

- The dog I received for Christmas when I was six
- The time my father fixed my car without complaining
- The time I visited my uncle at his Army barracks
- Graduating near to top of my class in college

Since the negative pivot points had weighed so heavily in Jim's life, he didn't think he had anything positive to contribute to himself. But by making a conscious effort to find his positive pivot points, as well as negative ones, he was able to give his emotional life some balance. I said to Jim what I will say to you: when trying to stop the struggle, it is very important to find your positive pivot points. Because the negative pivot points carry more authority than the positive ones, they tend to blot out the good things in your life the way an eclipse blots out the sun. But, you have to remember that the sun is still there, you just have to look a little harder to see it. And the only way to do that, is to find those elusive positive moments in your life and learn how to savor them.

Awareness is the key in using our pivot points. In fact, awareness requires us to use them, if we truly want to make positive change in our own lives. Once we become aware how those specific events in the past have had an effect on our future, then common sense calls for us to use them to our advantage. If we don't do that, negative pivot points can fester and positive pivot points can be forgotten, and the opportunity to use their positive force lost.

Exploring Your Pivot Points, Negative And Positive

Negative pivot points are almost always at the root of struggle.

I can say with assurance that all of the patients I've treated who are in the midst of struggle have pivot points that are related to the six categories of struggle: anger, fear, addiction, shame, excessive desire for status or money, and toxic need for love and/or acceptance. And I can also say that I have struggled with many of these sources of pain myself. We all have. Hence, the *Get A Grip* books I have written on each of these subjects.

The goal in this book is to bring the struggle back into balance, or eliminate it completely. Doing this is not an easy task, given that negative pivot points generally involve negative events with formidable people that determine how we see ourselves, or react to the world around us. They are events that have impressed some kind of negative behavior in our psyche, that is either aggressive or submissive.

I've already made it clear that finding and confronting your pivot points can lead to a breakthrough to a higher power; that place where you no longer feel uncomfortable with yourself but don't really know why. But how is it that you clearly define your pivot points? And what do you do with your pivot points – the good and the bad ones – when you discover what they are?

These two questions are the very crux of this book. But the first question you might have is: how do I clearly define my pivot points? To answer this question, I will go back to Jim and show you the techniques I used with him.

The Goal: Discovering Your Pivot Points

The goal of this chapter is to create a list of pivot points, first the negative ones (because they are usually close to the surface), and then the positive ones, which are less obvious and usually more difficult to ferret out. There is a third type, labelled "never to be opened" because these take careful navigation to open. Only when we are ready, and at times with guidance, we can open them.

Some people know right away what their pivot points are and need no help in listing them. They know that something in their past is causing them to struggle in the present, and they are able to see them clearly once the concept is presented to them. Still others just need to talk about their lives with a therapist, or even a trusted friend, before they come up with a useful list of the things that are making them struggle. Then there are the difficult ones, patients who understand the concept of pivot points but have spent a lot of time denying them and need extra help. This goal is aimed at those who have a great amount of difficulty discovering, or even exploring, their pivot points.

It may seem ridiculous to you that a person can't look back and see painful or humiliating events that have helped shape their life. Yet there are many who can't. They have spent so much time closeting them in their mind, or trying to reshape them into positive events, that they can no longer see or conceive that they were negative, let alone pivotal. The person who tells you that his father was nice yet a strict disciplinarian, is usually talking around the fact that he was beaten or verbally abused as a child. A woman who declares that her husband had a right to hit her, is definitely trying to reshape a negative pivot point into something she can accept. Or the person who justifies over-drinking by saying daily, that he had a stressful day at work. And on and on.

People who live in such denial are struggling with something they have tried very hard not to look at. What might that be? They sometimes honestly don't know because their mind is cleverly trying to protect itself from the pain of self-analysis.

There are many ways to help them discover the source of their struggle. I have already mentioned two. Just the process of describing what pivot points are is all it takes for some people. And, of course, talking with a therapist or a friend will sometimes do it. Another story of self-discovery came from the wife of a serious alcoholic who had learned to drink from his alcoholic father, and had drank hard through their 14-year marriage. This woman told me that she had begged her husband to stop drinking since before they were married, and nothing she said made him stop, in fact it only egged him on. When she asked him to stop drinking, he would angrily declare that she reminded him of his mother, who nagged his father to stop drinking all of his life.

Then one day he became so drunk that he collapsed on the street. Dozens of people walked by as he struggled to get up. Then a well-dressed man stepped out of the passing crowd and picked him up off the sidewalk.

The man helped him walk to a bus stop and managed to get him to sit down. Then he looked her husband in the eye and said with the greatest of kindness, "How long have you been a drunk?"

With that, the woman said her husband's life flashed before him. And from that day forward – 10 years later when she told me the story – he never drank again.

These flashes of insight happen to some people; but for most there is a process one must go through to gain insight. Since negative pivot points occur around specific behaviors - anger, fear, addiction, shame, or the desire for status, money, love or acceptance - a person searching for the cause of one of these behaviors will have the best result finding their negative pivot points when one of these behaviors breaks out. For example, an unexplained outburst of anger would be the time to search for the deep source of that anger. A sudden outburst of unexplained fear would be the time to take a break and ask yourself, "What am I fearful of?" A fit of uncontrolled spending on an unnecessary luxury item would be the time to ask yourself whether you spent that money just to impress others…and so on. There are many negative behaviors in our lives that can be set off by pivot points. That's why it's important to take a break when these events take place, and discover why they have taken place. In my experience, that is the best way to stop the struggle.

The technique I have found most effective in discovering these pivot points is that of guided meditation. Most meditation is passive, in the sense that you assume a comfortable position and attempt to clear your mind of all thought and judgment. If a thought or judgment arises in your mind, as it usually does during meditation, you are supposed to "let it go", which means to not ponder or judge it, rather let it pass from your mind.

Guided meditation in the search of negative pivot points is very different. It calls for you to focus deeply on your emotional state for the purpose of analyzing that state, the source of your struggle.

Guided meditation can be uncomfortable for some who may find themselves reliving some very distressing moments in their lifetime. But the beauty of guided meditation is that you get to relive these moments alone, and are able to recall them only to yourself and not to others around you. Think about that, you are able to recall the most uncomfortable moments in your lives – those negative pivot points – and then respond to them the way you wish you had responded when they happened. With this form of meditation, you can literally reframe an event by seeing yourself doing what you should have done in the beginning. By doing this, you take the negative power out of the event.

The act of reframing these events allows for the edge to be taken from them. Perhaps it has to do with a person facing the source of their struggle at a time in their life when they are older and more capable of responding properly.

I have had patients who have largely left their struggles behind after a single session of guided meditation that allowed them to experience the pivot point again. Why is this? Because the mind is more powerful than reality. A person who can successfully reframe a negative event from their childhood – understanding why it happened and how they can now change it from their adult perspective – can provide an understanding of events that take the power out of the pivot point. As one patient said, "Guided meditation allowed me to understand my mother's frame of mind when she spoke abusively to me. Reliving this as an adult allowed me to understand the other things that were going on in her life. Once I did that, I no longer took her abuse personally. I understood that it was not all aimed at me but at other things in her life as well."

Many who practice guided meditation have comments like this. Exploring pivot points from the perspective of age allows one to understand so much more than could be understood as a tender child. There is a CD, or downloadable audio file, on my website called the *Wise Old Being Meditation* which can help you with this.

Questions and Answers

Question: How do I do guided meditation?

Answer: Since it is so much easier to follow meditation as a guide reads it, than to read it yourself, I have created a number of meditations on my website that you can listen to.

Question: What if guided meditation doesn't work, or worse, if I can't handle it?

Answer: Guided meditation allows you to build up positive pictures, thoughts, or memories in your mind. When you build them, they actually outweigh the dark areas that are called negative pivot points.

Question: When people discover their negative pivot points, what are they supposed to do with them? A person can feel pretty raw when they discover the source of their struggle.

Answer: Once a person discovers their negative pivot points, they are able to see the root cause of negative actions in their lives. To acknowledge that you survived those incidents, you must have tools like the meditations, and other suggestions presented in this book, that allow you to make changes and live a happier and healthier life.

Question: Let's talk about negative pivot points. I've had many positive things happen in my life but, like Jim in this chapter, I seem to focus on the negative. Why do negative events stick in our heads so much more than the positive ones?

Answer: The answer to this is easy, and yet very compli-
cated. The fact of the matter is, that when we experience a
negative incident, the emotions behind the negative event
are far stronger – betrayal, abandonment, fear, resentment,
disappointment, grudges – than a positive event. There's
so much more energy behind a negative pivot point, that
it becomes a powerful negative charge of emotion…that's
life. It takes more mental energy to beat a negative emotion, than to bring a positive one into our heart. The rule
here: love always wins.

To patients I say this:

- **Persistence** equals making the conscious effort
  to continue
- **Knowledge** equals your goal, why you are persisting, what you want to achieve
- **Self-Love** equals realizations, what is needed to
  keep going and achieve your goal

CHAPTER 2

The Patient I Never Had

"You yourself, as much as anybody in the entire universe, deserve your love and affection." Siddhārtha Gautama

Lesson: How To Travel the Path to Self-Love

The patient who haunts me the most is one I never treated. He was my brother Brian, and he struggled mightily with life.

Ironically, his struggle with life stopped on the day of his greatest victory. He was on the courthouse steps after winning a settlement against the school for juvenile delinquents, where priests had sexually abused him, when he clutched his chest in pain. A few hours later he was in a coma. A few days later he was dead. His big, misunderstood heart stopped in 2004.

Brian's life was a tragic series of events that overwhelmed him. The first took place when he was about nine years of age. Brian was walking down a Dublin street when he noticed that the delivery bicycle belonging to the local butcher was not chained to the post. Rather than continue walking, Brian hopped on the bike and rode it to the bakery shop where he was going, about two blocks away. When he came out of the shop with a loaf of bread tucked under his arm, a policeman nabbed him by the collar and took him to jail.

That simple arrest for "borrowing" a delivery bike (Brian said he was going to return it on his ride back) led him to children's court where the judge slammed his gavel, gave him six months in the Letterfrack Catholic juvenile home, and then dismissed him to the bailiff to get on with his next case.

A few weeks later, Brian showed up at home, looking dazed and frightened. He had escaped from "the hell hole", he declared to my mother, and swore he would not go back.

What he didn't tell mom – couldn't tell her – was that a priest at the juvenile home was raping him. Every day a Christian brother would visit Brian in the dorm and take him to a private office. Then, as he buggered my brother, and he beat him with a stick for the sin of letting him do this to him. It made no sense. It didn't have to...and it wasn't Brian's fault, but he really didn't know that. All Brian knew was that he didn't want to go back to the juvenile home.

Mom sent him back. She didn't know what was taking place. All she knew was that an educated judge had deemed him a low-level criminal and sentenced him to a well-known Catholic industrial school. "Maybe he would return a better boy than the one who left", she said.

Of course, that wasn't possible, as years later the government investigated and found the school to be rife with physical and sexual abuse. The government report declared that 147 children had died while in the care of the Christian Brothers, mostly from abuse and neglect. The report found that the main means of control was "severe, excessive and pervasive" corporal punishment that was aimed at creating a climate of fear. And sexual abuse was prevalent. The report found that many of the priests at Letterfrack were known sexual abusers, but were not investigated or dismissed by the brotherhood. Instead, the abuse of these boys was allowed to persist for the life of the school, "unprotected in a hostile environment isolated from their families", as the report declared. When they left this hellish institution, they did so with little education, no adequate training to become productive citizens, and no knowledge of how to cope socially with the normal world.

Brian was returned to that environment where he was beaten and buggered for six more months. When he returned home, he was a different person; one who struggled enormously.

School meant nothing to him. He completed elementary school and then ran aground and gave up in secondary school. All Brian wanted to do was spend the day inside the four walls of his bedroom, safe from the outside world and any other pedophiles that could get to him. It was typical panic attack behavior, in which a person stays well within their comfort zone, and experiences deep anxiety about leaving it. For Brian, his comfort zone was the world before his sexual abuse. He never really grew up beyond that. He would spend the day playing records, looking at magazines, and drinking.

In fact, it was the drinking that allowed Brian to leave his comfort zone occasionally. He was a creature of the night, roaming the streets and clubs of Dublin with other victims of poverty; as well as those who had been broken by a cruel juvenile court system. One that was eventually shown by government investigators, to be at the root of a social disease of poverty and cruelty that was ruining Ireland.

I realize now, that night gave my brother Brian anonymity. When he went out into the darkness, people could not see the type of person Brian was, a frightened little boy with a huge and painful secret that he thought would be visible to all who saw him in the light of day. He drank copious amounts of alcohol on these nights out, and when that wasn't enough to numb the pain of a past that haunted him, he began to take drugs. He took speed to stay awake through the long nights, and then downers in the early morning to put an end to them. He lived like a vampire, sleeping by day, and carousing by night. And, like a vampire, he preyed on people at night, too.

Brian learned a variety of ways to scam, steal, even bully money out of people. He carried drugs for dealers so they wouldn't be the ones caught with the goods if stopped by the police. He stole anything he could sell – cars, clothing, boxes of goods off trucks, milk off doorsteps, cigarettes, candy – anything. He was known to strong-arm the weak, grab cash from the registers of unwary shop owners, and flee from restaurants when the dinner bill arrived. Brian was a one-man crime wave, out of control.

He lived this way because he was haunted by the horror of being raped by authority figures that were supposed to help him, and also by being abandoned by those who had sworn to protect him, including, I'm afraid, his own family.

Rather than listen to the torture Brian had been through at the juvenile home, my parents were nowhere to be found when their second eldest son began talking about his nightmare. Mom was an alcoholic who spent all day in a booze-induced haze. And Dad was nowhere to be found when his son started talking. He would change the subject or just leave the room, because like most Irish men of his generation, he couldn't accept that the Holy Roman Church was guilty of such heinous crimes.

Only one time do I remember the subject of Brian's sexual abuse coming up in a family situation. It happened when I, myself, was abused by a teacher. I was at the kitchen table with Brian and Dad when I decided to reveal that a teacher at school had touched me inappropriately. Dad couldn't – wouldn't – believe it. He began to argue that a teacher would never do such a thing. That was when Brian arose from the dead (which is how he looked in the morning), and said with great authority, "For fucksake Dad, listen to him. It's happening all over this country."

An uncomfortable silence fell over the room, as my father listened to my story. Had something like this happened to him? I wondered. If so, it would have explained a lot about our family's dysfunction. And, it certainly explained a lot about Brian's deterioration over the years.

He had no one to talk to ever about what had happened to him at Letterfrack. Instead, he kept the pain of those abusive months inside, where it festered and took over his heart and mind.

Brian hated authority and fought it incessantly.

One night, for example, he picked me up in a car I had never before seen and suggested we drive around a while. Soon the flashing lights of a police car were on our tail. We pulled over and Brian looked at me with a seriousness I can see to this day.

"This is a stolen car, Derek. Just pretend you are deaf and mute, and everything will be okay. Don't say a word!"

I stared straight ahead as Brian apologized for having no tags, registration, or proof of insurance in the car.

"I wouldn't be driving this car if my brother wasn't deaf and dumb," he said to the policeman. But I need to get him back to his school, or he'll get very upset."

I took that as a cue and began to cry, silently at first, and then sobbing and shaking. Brian began to sign language me, as I was supposed to be deaf and dumb, I made hand gestures back as if we were communicating. The policeman melted with sympathy.

"Take it easy young man. We'll get you back right away."

The policeman returned Brian's license and went back to his car.

"Don't worry, young man," he said to me when he left. "Thank you," I uttered without thinking.

Somehow the fact that I spoke – the deaf-mute passenger spoke! – didn't register with the policeman. As he drove off, we howled with laughter.

Brian considered my performance *Oscar-winning* and insisted that we go out for dinner.

We drove into a strange neighborhood until we found a Chinese restaurant. Brian parked at the end of the street and we walked back to the restaurant. I had never seen Brian order so much food, nor relish in my company so much, as we talked about the event that had just taken place. With empty platters all around us, Brian began to fish through his pockets for cigarettes.

"Derek, I left my cigarettes in the car. Can you go get my jacket?"

Like a good brother I bounced up and headed for the car. No sooner had I opened the door and reached into the back seat for the jacket, did I feel a rough hand push me into the car and heard the door shut behind me.

I didn't have to ask why that series of events had taken place. Brian had stolen a meal and he was damned proud of it. As the Chinese owners ran up the street toward the car, Brian laughed, popped the car in gear and took off. He continued to laugh all the way home.

* * *

On the other hand, I didn't laugh at all. I was 15 and Brian was 25. Of my four brothers, he was the one that I had the most compassion and time for, but he was also the person I least wanted to be like. His heart had two sides: the big beautiful one, and the one that was dark and filled with all of the horrible things he wanted to hide. I loved the big heart, because it was what I wanted him to have all of the time. But, I was intrigued with the dark heart too, because it contained things like guilt, shame, anger, hate and other elements so painful, that he was driven to numb it with every substance possible.

In short, he was fighting hard to stop the struggle, but he had no tools with which to do it.

It was through Brian that I became aware of the large number of people around me who were trying to stop the struggle too. It was by knowing Brian, and observing his dark heart, that I could see the same struggle in those who were close to me. I could see it in my mother, who started drinking the day she discovered my father in bed with her best friend. She was struggling for love. I could see it in Brian, who could not speak about the rape and physical abuse he had experienced. He was struggling to be heard. I could see it in the face of my father, who was struggling about the way he had treated our mother. He was struggling with guilt. I could even see it in the lives of my "tribe," a group of 60 or so boys, of whom very few have defied drug and alcohol addiction in the decades since our childhood. In a world of poverty, they were struggling for equality.

And so on. There was a lot of struggle going on, but most of it was never discussed. People rarely address their struggles head-on. Instead, they deal with them silently, or in a code that they don't truly understand themselves, but that almost always relates to numbing the pain. It makes a guessing game of what is causing the struggle, and sometimes it results in habits that become so ingrained, that the person doesn't know where they come from. So, for example, my mother began drinking to kill the pain she experienced when she found my father and her best friend half-naked and rushing to get dressed. She remembered discovering the tryst between my father and her friend, but she no longer linked it with her drinking. It was as though the drinking had started on its own. It was only deep in her psyche that she linked the infidelity with drinking, and let's face it, she drank to keep from going there.

The same was true of my father. He became a terribly angry man after the affair was uncovered. I had difficulty being around him most of the time because he would explode in rage over the slightest of things. It was as though the anger had a life of its own, independent of the illicit affair itself. Yet his anger was directly linked to the infidelity. But like my mother, he kept that event deep in his psyche where it festered, and manifested itself in general anger.

And so on. My brother was so damaged by the pain and shame of being raped by the Christian Brothers, and so concerned others would blame him for the crimes of his keepers, that he was unable to speak about what had happened. His struggle caused psychic pain, too, the kind that kept him from being able to speak about it. The silence he couldn't break became the reason for drinking and drugging; and the hatred he felt for authority became the reason he made his meager living as a crook. And my friends and I were too proud and afraid to admit to one another that we deeply feared the life of lack we had been born into, and that the only way out was education and clear thinking. Instead we thought, being tough, noisy and drunk was the path to success and equality. Soon, many of my friends closeted the notion of equality, and became bitter about it actually. They rarely dealt with the path to success. As they aged, they felt that path had closed, and that equality was impossible. And they were right. At that point, equality became unattainable, and they numbed the pain of this realization with drugs and alcohol. They had given up.

All of the people mentioned above had a struggle. None of them could stop it. I dare say, that most wouldn't even know what I meant if I asked, "Have you been able to stop the struggle?" And you, would you know what I meant if I said to you, "Have you been able to stop the struggle?"

Struggle, and potential struggles, are all around us. Nations struggle over boundaries, religious groups struggle for identity, politicians struggle for power. These are the struggles of the greater world that we as individuals have little power over.

The struggle I am talking about here, is the personal struggle. We, as individuals, struggle to be seen, to be loved, to be heard, to be confident, to be truthful, to get what we want, to get others to do what we want. The list of things we struggle for, about, and with seems almost endless. Many people wake up in the morning with struggle on their minds, live with it all day, and go to bed with it at night.

Many of these struggles come to us from our own sense of inadequacy. Sometimes, though, they are planted by the world around us. We struggle with fears about the future because these fears have been planted in us by politicians. We struggle with imperfections in our body because advertising on media tells us we don't look, dress, or smell right. On a daily basis, we are pelted by hundreds of media messages, many of which create a sense of struggle in our minds.

Since struggle, by its very definition, is a challenge or problem that requires strenuous mental or physical effort to overcome, it is no wonder that people with struggle in their lives feel bogged down, unable to progress. When that happens it can lead to a struggle over self, in which one asks, "Why am I unable to overcome all of the struggles in my life? "

These struggles can then lead to exhaustion, self-image problems, depression, addictions, and so on. And eventually, the struggle becomes so bad, you don't discuss it. The struggle becomes internalized, hidden behind bad habits that protect it and keep it from being tampered with.

Of course, the source of our struggles needs to be tampered with. Without careful tampering, the struggle stays with us always.

Which brings me back to Brian. He may not have used the word "struggle," but he knew he was struggling. He couldn't even leave his bedroom on most days, because he was afraid of the world around him. In fact, I once joked with him that his bedroom must be what the inside of his head looked like. It was filled with the items of his childhood – sports pictures, half-nude women in pin-up posters, shabby clothing, and a record collection that was the envy of the neighborhood. Most of the time the room looked like a bomb had hit it. And Brian sat on his bed right in the middle of it, smoking cigarettes and presiding over his disheveled kingdom.

"Why don't you go get some help from a doctor?" I asked.

Brian shook his head when I said that.

"They would put me in the nut house," he said. "If people like me complain about their problems, they just put them in an institution and throw away the key."

He must have done some research because it proved that he was, in fact, correct. A person who went to counseling 45 years ago in Ireland, was considered mad. Even up to 35 years ago, a person who went to counseling for anxiety, ran a good chance of being diagnosed with having a "nervous breakdown." The same would be true of someone who was an alcoholic, or even a mother who was worried about her children. "Nervous breakdown" was the standard diagnosis for all such issues, and such a diagnosis could easily put a person into an institution.

"Of course, I could always go see a priest!" he said, laughing. "They are more than willing to help boys like me."

I felt myself blush when he said that. He had told me some of what happened to him in Letterfrack. I don't think he ever told anyone all of what happened to him at that institution; and the mere mention of a priest by my brother, conjured horrible images for me. I couldn't look at him after that.

I was a teenager when this was going on. And in many ways, Brian was the reason I decided to become a psychotherapist. I had a deep need to understand the issues that had affected him, and, for that matter, the issues that affected my entire family. Perhaps the better word would be 'infected' my entire family. Despite being revered in the neighborhood as a model family (some even called us *The Waltons*, for being so similar to the idealized farm family portrayed on the television series of the same name), we were very far from perfect. Like so many families that are thought to be exceptional, but aren't, we were just quiet. We kept to ourselves, and kept the secrets of what happened behind closed doors.

If we hadn't been so quiet, the neighbors would have discovered that my mother was a raging alcoholic, who began drinking in the morning and was often blacked-out by evening. They would have known that my father was a rageaholic, a man with deep issues that led him to anger. They would have noticed that Brian wasn't working the night shift in a factory, which is what my mother told the neighbors when asked why he was home in the afternoon.

Our family was far from being *The Waltons*. But it was very good at living the lie instead of living the life. As one of my other brothers said, "If the neighbors knew the truth, they would think we were the *Addams Family*." Don't get me wrong, we had great moments too, that were like *The Waltons*. My brothers and sisters all supported each other in many ways.

One of my goals in life became the desire to understand my family members, and figure out what had made them the people they were. To do that, I decided to study psychotherapy.

I loved this field of study, I still do, because it gives me the keys to the universe that I want to explore. With the help of Freud, Jung, and other masters of therapy, I was able to explore the human psyche, like a watchmaker explores a watch, learning about the gears and springs that propel our conscious and subconscious minds.

But when I graduated from school and opened a practice in Dublin, I developed doubts about psychotherapy. To be sure, there is magic in talk therapy. By building a relationship of trust with a patient, and then carefully excavating their lives, one can uncover the many layers of their past and discover why certain behaviors exist.

Talk therapy is amazingly helpful in discovering childhood experiences that may drive a person's everyday behavior, especially if that person has never explored their own psyche for the causes of their behavior. But, I discovered that the vast majority of my patients were already aware of why they acted the way they did. It was like my brother Brian: he knew it was the sexual abuse by priests that made him a social misfit. He also knew that discussing it was painful and would always be so. In fact, he said that just thinking about it, was at times like hitting a nerve in a tooth with a dental drill. He didn't, necessarily, want to talk about it, but he did want to overcome the feelings of helplessness and worthlessness so he could get on with his life.

The same was true of other patients. Women who didn't trust their husbands, already knew about the infidelity of their fathers. Men who were always angry, remembered well being raised by angry fathers. Adults who drank too much alcohol when the going got tough, could recall their parents doing exactly the same thing. None of them needed me to dig back into their painful past. Rather, they needed resolution to the problem.

"It isn't that people don't know what their problems are," I told a psychology professor I respected. "It's that they don't know how to get over them. They just don't know how to stop the struggle."

I discussed my discovery with several professors and fellow therapists, and almost universally, the answer was to "keep searching". Rather than accept that the patient knew what his or her problem was, and was now ready for a resolution, most therapists suggested going deeper into their past. It seemed to be their common belief, that if a patient said they knew their problem, they probably didn't, and that somewhere in the dark recesses of their mind, the real problems were hidden and ready to come out, only if a therapist kept digging.

I didn't believe it.

I came to discover that it was traditional psychotherapy itself that was the problem. It had become ossified, frozen in the past. Most therapists were comfortable searching for a deep-seated issue in a person's life – the deeper the better – but would not commit to a solution of that issue. They just wanted to keep searching and searching, even though the frustrated patient had told them over and over what the true issue was.

I wanted to offer usable solutions, so the patients could get on with their lives. I began to search for those solutions on my own.

Sadly at times, the search I am talking about began in the dysfunctional family I was raised in, and then spread out to my patients, and then actually became a worldwide search, one that took me to India, where I discovered the valuable connections between Western and Eastern psychology. The search allowed me to explore the sources of all struggle – fear, anger, death, status, money, love, acceptance, addiction, shame – and the existential pain that takes place when a bad thing happens to a good person.

Searches like this one are largely based on answering questions that one finds along the way. In my search to find a way to stop personal struggle, I have written down many questions. And, I realized that a search like this never ends, and the questions never stop. So, I keep writing them down and trying to answer them, knowing now that this search is a lifetime journey I will never finish, just that it gets easier as you are going along.

But I did start somewhere. And the problems of Brian, my other siblings, and my parents, led me to write down my first questions:

Why does one sibling struggle with life while the others don't?

Why are some adults emotionally crippled? And, what can they do to change?

Are struggles an addiction? And do they really have to drive our lives?

And finally, are some people so mired in struggle that they are unreachable?

That last question is probably the most important one of all because it involves inertia, that tendency of a body at rest, to stay at rest. When I started developing techniques my patients could use to overcome their struggles, I realized that several of them resisted change entirely. They didn't want to stop the struggle. It was as though they had made a grudging friend with their struggle. Whether it was food addiction, fear, anger, or the host of other sources for struggle, they just didn't have the energy, or desire to move themselves out of the rut they were in, and move freely down another path.

Originally, I attributed this failure to change as being laziness. Patients came for change, and when they found it would take work, decided to sit back down until the desire for change passed. It was perplexing to me.

"People are just too lazy to make change and stop their struggle," I told Brian, who was one of those who understood my techniques, yet refused to use them.

"Some probably are too lazy, but then some people are too lazy to move out of the way of a speeding car," he said. "But remember... some people don't want to move out of the way of a speeding car."

"What do you mean?" I asked Brian, who could at times be very cryptic.

"I mean that some people are very comfortable seeing disaster coming. Some people like the pain. Some people have learned to live with it, and now it's the only thing they know," he said. "They don't want to move into the unknown because, well, it's something they don't know, like the saying "the devil you know is better than the devil you don't know.""

That strange piece of wisdom gets a lot of laughs from patients. Sometimes those laughs are uncomfortable ones. They know that personal change is movement into the unknown, which is something most people who are trying to stop their struggle deeply fear. To paraphrase Brian, people who can't stop the struggle have learned to live with the pain. Ultimately, they chose to not make a change for the better.

Not making positive change can often be a patient's choice. But if you are willing to move through this unknown, I promise an enlightenment that will take you far beyond normal, and give you personal power that you never thought possible.

Patients say that stopping their struggle is like having a spiritual experience, one that moves them beyond the improved world they expected to be in, and into a world of much greater possibilities. For example, if you have learned to control your anger using my techniques, you will feel more in control of your world, and people around you, because you will suddenly have a new level of respect from those who knew your former self. And if you struggle with a fear of life, you will find yourself free of that rut, and suddenly ready to experience the world as a fearless human being.

Patients of mine have found that the meditation techniques in this book put them in touch with a force outside of their body, one they describe as spiritual, or supernatural. No longer will you feel anchored by the source of your struggle. You will instead be free of the emotional baggage that has held you down. You will move from a world of few possibilities, into a world where all things seem possible.

I know this sounds like an impossible promise, but it's not. I have seen my patients go far beyond their expectations and into a world of great realizations, where struggle is replaced by confidence and control, and where fear and doubt are replaced by happiness and a sense of unlimited possibilities. They have become the captains of their fate, and so can you.

The Path To Personal Change Begins With Conscious Effort

No matter what your struggle is about – fear, anger, death, need for status and money, constant desire for love and acceptance, the pain of addiction and shame – the path to personal change begins with conscious effort. Conscious effort goes beyond knowing the source of personal struggle, and the knowledge of how to overcome it. Conscious effort is persistence. Without the conscious effort, overcoming struggle is just daydreaming. Conscious effort means you become your own guide, and being your own guide implies that you are on a path, moving forward to firmer ground, and out of the mire. Conscious effort means forward motion.

My brother Brian never was able to become the captain of his own fate, and perhaps with good reason. What happened to Brian – molestation by authority figures – is often a source of shame that leads to a downward spiral, and into addictions, phobias, and other psychological issues. People in shame are often emotionally frozen. It is conscious effort that keeps them from bottoming out.

Brian was never open to positive self-examination because it was painful for him to relive the incidents of abuse that had broken him as a young man. In fact, the abuse had made him so psychotic that he jumped out of the hospital window and ended up being told that he would probably not walk again because the injuries he sustained were for life. When he awoke from surgery, he thought the doctors were priests from Letterfrack come to molest him again, because of the heavy medications he was on. Brian could have stopped the struggle, but he didn't want to. He couldn't. He knew that doing so would mean having to relive the painful events in his life in a very deep and therapeutic way. Although there was no question in my mind that he relived these events on a daily basis, he also masked the pain of doing so with alcohol and drugs and by staying in his bedroom, or other "safe" places that represented his comfort zone. To actually dissect his issues, in front of a therapist, would be too much for Brian, as it is for many who struggle. For them, even the best psychologist or healer, cannot bring them out of their shell of safety.

But had he been amenable to self-examination, and if he had accepted my help, I would have helped him acknowledge his pain, as well as his strength for having survived. Then I would have spoken to the family, to see if anyone else would be willing to do the same.

Once those steps were done, and I felt there was some level of foundation there, I would start with some simple questions: Now what, Brian? Now what do you want? No matter how powerful you are, you cannot change the past. What would you like to change about your future if anything?

That's where the notion of conscious effort would have come in. No matter what the struggle involves, conscious effort to stop it is at the very forefront of the fight for freedom.

So, what is involved in conscious effort? Persistence, knowledge and self-love is the simple answer. Almost anything with the word "effort" in the title requires persistence, which is merely the ability to sustain effort. And of course, knowledge is a key ingredient, because it tells you why you are persisting and what it is you will receive for your persistence. It is knowledge that clarifies the path to the endgame. It lets you know what your goal is and how to get there.

But persistence and knowledge are not enough to power you up the path to change. Self-love is a necessary element because without it, conscious effort is usually too difficult to achieve, and with it, life becomes much easier.

So how do you assemble the right mixture of persistence, knowledge, and self-love? Oddly enough, it will all come if you can just master self-love.

Mastering Self-Love

It's almost laughable to say, "if you can just master self-love," because self-love is one of the most difficult things for mankind to master.

The notion of self-love is easy to misunderstand. When I mention self-love, you might be thinking of those extremely unpleasant and self-obsessed people who over-talk in groups, and aren't afraid to remind you of how great they are. I'm not talking about that kind of self-love. Those are generally insecure people who constantly have to pump up their ego to function in their world. When I talk about self-love, I am talking about people who have had the courage to explore their flaws as honestly as they can, and have come away with a love of themselves that allows them to continue to improve with confidence. We all struggle, but no matter what we struggle with, the struggle is first rooted in a lack of love for ourselves.

This may be confusing, especially if we believe that someone else did us wrong and we can blame our personal struggles on them. But the fact is, that the lack of self-love is only fixed if we make peace with ourselves. So, despite the painful fact that Brian was raped by the authority figures who should have been caring for him, in the end it was Brian who had to make peace with his feelings. The people who had abused him were dead and gone. The system that had failed him, didn't truly care that it had failed. The parents who had let him down were too ashamed to discuss their failures. That was it, if he didn't make peace with himself, there would be no peace.

What he didn't understand was what Buddha said about inner peace, "Peace comes from within, do not seek it without". I will go one further and say, that no matter what your source of struggle, it will always be there if you are not at peace with the person you should love the most, yourself. That is why I have chosen to make Mastering of Self-Love the first and foremost skill one must have in facing the struggles of life, because it will allow you to accept whatever you might find in your search to stop the struggle. Self-love is a force, the very underpinning you need to press forward. To stop the struggle, it is absolutely essential, that you first develop a self-love that can be the foundation of a new confidence.

In my decades as a therapist, I have helped patients develop self-love by giving them three tools. I call these Brian's Way, not because they represent the way chosen by my brother Brian, but – ironically – because they represent the path not taken, the one that would have led him to inner peace and a longer and happier life. Here they are:

Explore Yourself

Do you really know yourself? Are you really honest about who you are? Most people are not. There are thoughts and feelings inside of us, that we don't feel comfortable examining, which is too bad, since those are probably the thoughts and feelings that cause problems and are probably responsible for our lack of self-love. Yet to live free of self-loathing, we have to explore our thoughts and feelings, and accept our imperfections and faults. Why? Because self-examination is the key to self-acceptance. As an exercise, make a list of these secret head-talks you are having with yourself and then change the narrative.

Easier said than done, right? As one of my patients said to me, "There are a lot of dark rooms in my mansion that I don't like to go into because I'm afraid of the ghosts."

So be it. But still you need to shine that purifying light into those dark places, because that's the only way to get rid of the ghosts. It is only through this self-observation, that one is able to live free of the emotional obstacles that create self-loathing.

Once again, I know this is difficult. Honest self-exploration always is. But the beauty of self-exploration is that it can be done by yourself, and with yourself, and doesn't require that you share the painful information with anybody.

Forgive, Forgive, Forgive

The self-exploration exercise above, can easily result in

a list of grievances about yourself and others. If you are lucky, some of these grievances can be discussed with the person who is the source of the grievance. Many of my patients, for example, have issues with their parents that they have been able to discuss with them, others with spouses or partners. It is always gratifying to be able to talk about past issues and reach a resolution with that person.

But sometimes those people you would like to confront are not physically or mentally available themselves. They may be long gone, or no longer interested in your emotional well-being, or they may live in a world of denial about things they have done to people...that's how it was for my brother Brian. Had he been able to consciously explore his issues, I am sure he would have liked nothing more than to confront the rapist priests of Letterfrack with some hard questions.

I can promise that this conversation would have been very unsatisfying for Brian. The priests who were convicted lived in such a state of denial that they would have denied Brian's accusations. It would be like talking to a brick wall.

That brick wall of denial rises around many who are confronted with their wrongdoings. Admissions of guilt don't come easy, if at all, from most people, especially if those accusations are particularly heinous. This is why I tell my patients, your ability to forgive, if possible, those who have done you wrong, has to come from inside you. An exercise for this is to write a letter to the person, a letter that you never have to post, but express all of your emotions in it. A sense of satisfaction that you will get from this exercise, to forgive them their trespasses, will, actually, unlock a prison you have put yourself in by holding onto the anger.

I know this seems like a contradictory response for some. After all, isn't an admission of guilt the point of confronting the perpetrator? Don't you want to see them hang their head and apologize? What if it doesn't happen? What if they say, they don't know what you are talking about, or they have a different interpretation of what happened than you do? That could easily happen given the nature of memory...and then what?

That is one reason why, you need to plan to forgive the guilty party, no matter how hurtful their trespass might be. And it might be best to remember Mahatma Gandhi's feelings on forgiveness, which he summarized in this poignant quotation:

> "The weak can never forgive. Forgiveness is
> the attribute of the strong."

Accept Yourself

To accept yourself means to accept your imperfections, faults and all, and to quit hanging on to feelings of unworthiness. It also means to forgive others. Forgiveness of others removes an emotional weight from your shoulders. Had Brian done that with the evil people who tormented him, I am certain his life would have been greatly improved. After all, forgiveness heals most of the emotional wounds and keeps them from festering inside of you. But another tool to achieving self-love is to accept yourself...imperfections and all.

From watching Brian, I know that such an act of self-acceptance is extremely difficult. But if you can work on forgiving others, you can certainly work on forgiving yourself.

I don't mean to minimize the effort that can go into an individual's battle for self-acceptance. For some, life's biggest struggle might be the battle to accept one's own faults and imperfections. And in the course of avoiding those faults, you may build emotional walls that protect your true self from friends, wives, children, even yourself…for a while, at least. The fact is, that the person without self-love will have to take a journey inward to find it. They will have to surrender to the fact that they have committed trespasses in their own lives, too. There is no comfort in knowing that you might have to dive into a pool of personal grief to come away feeling good about yourself. Ralph Waldo Emerson summed it up when he said, "What lies behind us and what lies before us are tiny matters compared to what lies within us". When I read that, I see it as both a reason for self-examination, and a reason to avoid self-examination.

Still, I came to the conclusion that self-examination is the path to self-acceptance. One needs to quit hanging on to their unworthiness. It is not possible to build happiness with feelings of self-loathing. You need to look inside yourself, accept what you see, and forgive yourself. Change will come next, and then healing.

As you read this book and explore other solutions to life's struggles, you might refer back to the advice in this chapter as a refresher course in building the foundation of self-love that will help expand your life in ways that will make you a better leader, better parent and better friend, to others as well as to yourself. As far as I'm concerned, that is half the struggle right there.

I wish Brian had known that.

Questions and Answers

Question: Why can the thoughtless or cruel acts of others cause us to lose love for ourselves? After all, we know when we are victims of these acts. Why can't we just let them roll off our backs?

Answer: Usually the people who are carrying out those thoughtless or cruel acts are our superiors so we actually feel they are correct. When they disrespect us, we lose the foundation of who we are and what we are. If this person is cruel enough, they may even turn into a bully, making our lives even worse.

Question: I know that my issues revolve around a lack of self-love. I was verbally abused as a child by an angry father and was not protected by my mother. Yet I still take the blame for them. Why?

Answer: To begin with, congratulations because you have actually accepted that these events have happened. The next part is to stop blaming yourself…it's not your fault. Saying that you had an angry father, or an angry mother, is wonderful if they acknowledge their actions, but they usually don't. Most often, you just have to take back your power. And the best way for you to take back your power is to acknowledge that the past is the past. It can't be changed, but what can be changed, is the future. A well-planned life is about using what you know to change the future.

Question: I had a great childhood and have always had supportive friends and family. I'm happily married, educated and have a good job. Yet I lack self-love. Can someone be born with a lack of self-love?

Answer: Scientific evidence now backs up that children in the womb can be affected by negative vibes from their parents, their environment, and the ecology they're in, and actually have that built up prior to them even being born. Yes, you can feel unwelcome and unwanted as a child before you even arrive. That could be a root cause for lack of self-love.

Question: How can I stop blaming myself for the actions of others and start loving myself again? Are there techniques you can give me?

Answer: Again, we have to understand, that the actions of others are in the past. It is only if we allow those actions to continue to be a pattern, that we will then never break the cycle. So, actually, what we have to do, is find techniques and tools in order to break those patterns, first on an unconscious, and then a conscious level.

There are many ways to break those patterns. One is to close your eyes and imagine the offending person, and then imagine them wearing something foolish like Mickey Mouse ears, and when they talk, imagine their voice sounding squeaky like Mickey Mouse. Or, if it's a man, wearing a French maid's costume, with fishnet stockings and high heels.

Remaking these demons in your life overrides old patterns. If you do that a few times, the person ceases to be a serious threat. You may even laugh when they try to bully you. That's good, nothing breaks a bully like not being taken seriously. This is an NLP technique called reframing that overrides the old program, even helping to change the negative to a positive.

Another way to defeat the demons in your life, is to completely erase them from your mind for a period of time. One method of doing this is regular and determined exercise. My choice of exercise is martial arts. Because I am facing an opponent when I practice this discipline, I have to stay in the fight, be here now, or I will likely get defeated. Martial arts can truly be a metaphor for ignoring the past, and not needlessly pondering the future. To be competitive, you have to live in the now.

The same can be said of other forms of exercise, like yoga or running. These physical disciplines force one to live in the now.

Question: I am struggling with issues and know that's why I am reading this book. Is there a way to force a loved one to confront the harm they have done to me?

Answer: This is a very deep question. The first place to confront these actions is in your mind. That's important, because something that the mind sees it can actually achieve. Oftentimes, I've used such a technique with patients. I tell them to imagine themselves with a baseball bat, beating that person up. Surprisingly, eight out of 10 times, the person will turn around and say something like, "Do you know something, they're not worth it. I wouldn't bother beating them up." That becomes the beginning of the end for their issues.

In an odd way, this is a form of guided meditation, and a positive affirmation to reprogram your well-being. Again, what the mind sees it can achieve.

Question: It's painful to confront the issues that make me dislike myself. Is there a way to cope with these issues that isn't painful?

Answer: The best way to begin is to project the future. Realize you will feel free and liberated from pain, after you have confronted these issues. Stay focused on the endgame and see that the outcome far outweighs the pain that you may feel by confronting these issues.

Question: What is the most important thing to remember in making peace with one's self?

Answer: Making peace with yourself is about understanding that you're not perfect. That it's okay to make mistakes because it's through our mistakes that we actually learn who we are. And self-love is about loving all parts of yourself, warts and all, and understanding that if we can't achieve some level of self-love, then it's not possible for others to love us either. During the painful process of learning to love yourself, it's important to remember that self-love will then manifest powerfully in all aspects of your life.

CHAPTER 3

Finding a Higher Power

"When one door closes another door opens;
but we so often look so long and so regretfully
upon the closed door, that we do not see the
ones which open for us."
Alexander Graham Bell

When I was a teenager, I looked around me and saw a lot of people in chains. No, I don't mean literally in chains, but emotionally in chains.

Our house was always spotlessly clean because all of us children were scolded constantly by our mother to keep it that way. As a result, we did endless housework when we were home. Yet no matter how perfect the house looked, it was never good enough for her.

She not only complained about our housekeeping, she also told us how lucky we were to have what we have. She reminded us that her mother had died when she was only 10, and that her father and brothers insisted that she fill in the gap left by the loss. At this early age she gave up her childhood to become the mother of the house. Her position wasn't as royal as the one her mother occupied. If the house wasn't clean and dinner on the table when "the men" returned home from work, she would likely get the back of a hand from a demanding brother or even her father.

They worked as dockers, powerful men who wore wide leather belts for back support so they could carry heavy bags of cement down steep gangplanks from merchant ships. They were exhausted and hungry at the end of the day and were determined to control the only world they could, the one at home.

And, my mother told us, she was determined to do the same thing. We could count on a constant barrage of insults and abuse from our mother, who always found something wrong with the way we cleaned house. Some of my siblings are damaged to this day from her verbal abuse.

My parents were in emotional chains, too. They were not sleeping in the same room and seldom spoke a kind word between them. There was one thing they agreed on and that was discipline. They were demons for discipline, but mainly because they wanted to make sure that we were home and under control so they could go out and drink. And there was another reason, too. They wanted to make sure that our family had, the appearance at least, of being perfect.

This desire for perfection was a form of camouflage for my mother. Everyone in the neighborhood knew that there were some pretty dark issues in our household. Tales of infidelity and drinking don't stay secret long in Dublin neighborhoods. But my mother wasn't aware enough to know that. And besides, she was in competition with the family next door, a family she considered the most perfect in the neighborhood.

Of course, they weren't, but they put up a good front. Every day the kids were up early and out the door. When they finished school, they all got jobs and continued to get out of the house as quickly as they could to get to work. At night they would hang out on the curb until all hours, smoking cigarettes and speaking in hushed tones to one another. Even on Saturday mornings, when most people were sleeping a few extra hours, these kids were out the door and down the street.

My mother was impressed with this. She liked that they seemed driven to get to work and did so in unison, all of them leaving together as the mother walked them out the door. She wished we would do the same. Sometimes she would look out the window as they left and then turn to us as we lolled at the breakfast table.

"Look at you, you lazy group of good for nothings," she would say. "Why don't you get out there and get ahead like them?"

On Saturday morning she would swing the door to our bedroom open and demand that we get up. "The McMurray's are up. You need to get up and enjoy this day like they do. I should do what she does and walk you to the door."

With that, we generally rolled over and ignored her.

It wasn't until a few years later that word leaked out that the father was sexually abusing all of his children. When the mother discovered her husband's crimes, she began protecting her children by rounding them up in the morning and getting them out the door, telling them not to come back until late.

The stable and conscientious family she thought lived there turned out to be a fraud.

My mother was a strange woman. I remember a time when she completely defended me against a neighbor who caught me and some of my friends stealing a few strawberries from his back garden. We had been out camping overnight when one of my friends said, "Mr. Jones has an apple tree and strawberries in his garden, let's go get some." As we were in his garden at 5am in the morning, he looked out the window shouting "I know who you are. I'm going to your mothers and fathers." As we scattered, each running home to our own houses, I jumped into bed. Ten minutes later there was a banging on our front door. My parents woke up, my mother opened the door to the ranting and raging neighbor screaming about how Derek had stolen some strawberries. I was called down the stairs, standing there terrified that my mother was going to kill me. Something amazing happened, my mother stood up for me. She told the neighbor to get the fuck away from the door at this hour of the morning, screaming at him, "Are you serious? Banging down the door for a few strawberries, get a grip!", and slammed the door in his face. And turning to me she said, "Don't get caught again, now go to bed."

During these times, my mother would give things away as she was a very generous person at heart. If a neighbor needed a mattress, and couldn't afford to buy one, she would tell one of us to carry our mattress across the street. At the time I thought she had gone crazy. We didn't have much in the way of material goods, and to be giving things away like she was made very little sense to me, especially when she was giving away things that wouldn't be replaced for a while, like mattresses, furniture and clothing.

Later I realized that she had a deep need to feel valuable and loved and was feeling less of both in our household. None of us reached out to her anymore like we used to, so when neighbors mentioned specific needs, she was quick to help, if only to feel important and needed. Now I understand what was going on in her head. She was trying to break out of the depression caused by her emotional chains and feel better about herself. She was doing this in the only way that seemed practical at the time, by helping those who were reaching out for help. She was trying to find a higher power. What does that mean? To me now it means that she was trying to go beyond her limited world into a world with forces that could help her find a positive path in her life. For some this higher power is spiritual. It is a force that actually reaches outside of our head in prayer to seek answers from God. For others it is reaching deep inside of our mind with meditation, to change the way the brain reacts to certain stimuli, to make it a force for happiness and positive thinking. Some people use it by participating in AA groups, therapy groups or religious groups, and others go on an inner journey to find the root cause of their unhappiness, reassessing the events and looking for the positive, even within the negative, as in the yin being part of the yang, and the yang in the yin.

When I look back on this period in my mother's life with the knowledge I have now acquired, I think she felt seeking a higher power would make a difference. I also think she didn't have a clue as to how to find it. She was bound up in emotional chains that she couldn't, or wouldn't, break out of. Her universe was not a bright one, and every little blow to her reality caused it to darken just that much more. Soon she realized that her one-person charity wasn't giving her the emotional satisfaction she was seeking, and she withdrew just that much more. After that I never saw her happy again...much.

Her struggle seemed insurmountable and obvious to all of the children in the family. But we were teenagers and none of us had the knowledge to help her.

It was about this time that mom left the family. She was drinking a lot more and now spent the entire day in a boozy haze. At night she spent more and more time in bars with her friends. And as she did, she quit dressing up the way she used to. Her new and more destructive goal was to drink in the evening the way she had been drinking all day, and to do that she had to reduce the amount of "mirror time," putting on makeup so she would look good for the girls.

Then one day she came home and announced she was going to leave the country, spend five days a week at her sister's in England. My father's work hours had been cut back and there was less money at home. She was going to boost our family's economy by taking two jobs in England, she said, one at Madame Tussaud's Wax Museum and the other as a helper for a seamstress. And then she faded away. She took the ferry to England on Monday mornings and came home on Friday nights, just in time to go out with her friends and not come home until Saturday night. A quick wash of her clothing, a few hours sleep, and she was back on the ferry by Monday afternoon, ready for her stint as a ticket seller at the wax museum.

With the disappearance of mom, dad took on a greater physical presence in the house. He was downtrodden at this point, angry at himself for his philandering, depressed at the loss of his wife, and beaten down by his lack of full employment. His lack of self-esteem came out in volcanic bursts of anger, and at times when we least expected them. I remember working on simple projects around the house when I suddenly noticed a cold silence from my father as a distressed look would come across his face. Then, no matter what we were doing, he would find something to be angry about. Sometimes he would just destroy whatever it was we were working on, or he would berate me or my brothers, telling us that we were mechanically incompetent, or unable to focus on projects that would make our home a better place to live in. It was as though he thought we could pound a couple of nails in the wall, twist in a couple of screws, and all of the relationships in our family would be fixed, everything would be okay.

Each of us siblings had our own response to my father's anger. Brian, for instance, refused to have much of anything to do with dad. He had an occasional beer with him, and sometimes found himself in the kitchen at the same time dad came in for a bite to eat. But Brian spent most of his time in his room, and little time around either parent, both of whom had let him down when he needed them the most. My brother Des tried hard to breakthrough with both parents, but failing at that, he became a sad young man whose self-esteem diminished as his efforts to please our parents failed.

I like to think that I wasn't damaged by the lack of compassion and presence of my parents. I just went numb to the family scene. I realized there was little if any change I could affect in the lives of my parents, and I gave up on family life. I decided to seek my own path. And by seeking my own path, I truly mean my own path. I too wanted love and acceptance. Although, I didn't know it by name, I knew something was missing and I went in search of it.

I looked at my friends as possible role models and realized there was nothing there. Many of them were well on the path to addiction and crime, two things that had brought my older brother down. The prospect of becoming a shell of a human like Brian was a frightening notion for me. My other friends had little creativity and were followers, ready to do what others suggested, but rarely able to come up with anything interesting on their own. One or two had good prospects but they were the minority, not the majority.

I could no more change my parents than I could change my past. But I was desperate to change my future. I was only a teenager, but at several points in my life I had already tapped into events that told me there was a vast and important world out there, one that was invisible yet influential. By finding that world I could change my destiny.

I examined my young life and found several times in which I had been exposed to events that seemed to be otherworldly. If you look carefully and without cynicism at your own life, you will find many such events, too. Some seem to be psychic, or transcendent, or just moments of peace and tranquility in the midst of a storm. We tend to ignore these events, but they are important because they are moments when we have punched through to a higher plane and experienced life the way it could be.

As I said, I examined my own life and found several of these moments. First was an incident already recounted in which I had a profound feeling that my mother was going to be hurt or killed in a bus accident and I acted in a way to stop her from getting on that doomed bus.

There were other events. When I was twelve, I played hooky from school and went into Dublin. There, sitting at a bus stop in front of a hospital, I suddenly envisioned a child running into the street and being struck by a car. It was so vivid that my young heart jolted, and I sat up straight as a rod. About 15 minutes later, the actual event took place. A child ran down the sidewalk from the hospital and sprinted into the street without looking. She was struck hard by a passing car.

Pandemonium broke out as the parents and bystanders rushed into the street to care for the little girl. I stood there frozen. I had seen this event take place twice – once before it happened, and then when it actually happened – and I knew something extraordinary had taken place.

Recalling this event now, I see it as just one of the many times I had reached a higher plane, where time and space didn't seem to be linear.

I remembered other events. One of these happened with a boy who had just moved to town from Northern Ireland.

For reasons I don't understand, I was able to tap into his life so directly that within the first five minutes of meeting I not only told him his grandfather had recently died, I told him the grandfather's name, where he had worked, how he had died, and enough aspects of his life to totally freak out the new kid.

I didn't understand why these psychic moments happened. I did seem to share a psychic ability that was possessed by my mother and grandmother. But I liked having the ability because it added depth to my life, a sense that there was a lot going on that we could tap into if we chose to become quiet, introspective, and attentive to our thoughts. It was through these moments, that I came to the conclusion that, we had purchased a ticket to life but were only watching half the show. The other half was out there for all of us to see if we could keep the distractions of daily life from getting in the way.

Now, at the age of 15, I wanted to clarify my life, to concentrate on each precious moment and wring the life out of it. I wanted to find a higher power and I began to look for ways to get there. That was when I began to practice judo more powerfully, I had taken my first judo lesson at age 5 or 6.

Judo is a form of martial arts, defined in some dictionaries as a system of combat and self-defense. But I think martial arts go far beyond that simple definition, if for no other reason than it requires the practitioner to operate in the now. All sports – if done well – require the participant to "be in the now." To be a good runner, for instance, one must monitor heart rate and breathing almost constantly to avoid going too slow or too fast. Swimming requires the same discipline, as do team sports like soccer or baseball. To be a good athlete, living in the now is a requirement. If you slip into the past or try to think too far into the future, you may miss something that is going on right now. And in sports as in life, right now is the most important moment.

It was later when I realized that the power of living in the "now" kept the past from infecting my future. It has freed me to be in the moment, and connected me to the raw power of life, free of filters, which is a way in which most people are not connected. At the time, I didn't realize practicing judo would do such a thing for me. My real goal in becoming a martial artist was to be able to throw people around.

But it was this very fact – that I wanted to throw people around – that made martial arts such a powerful tool of "now-ness." I discovered that most people resist being thrown around. In fact, many of them shared my desire to throw others around. It was that very sense of opposing forces – yin and yang, as the Chinese say – that kept me totally focused on the now. If my mind drifted into the past, or went too far forward to a future move, I was likely to find myself upside down on a mat, wondering how I had gotten there.

To excel at judo required that I stay very firmly in the now when I needed to. And I did excel. My brother-in-law had introduced me to Judo/Martial Arts at age 5 or 6, I immediately loved it and took to it like a duck to water, excelling very quickly through the ranks. From Judo, I went on to practice many other martial arts like Karate, Taekwondo, Jujitsu, etc.

I remember one day the teacher of the club, Master Park, pulled me to one side as I was sparring, and gave me some advice that has stayed with me my entire life.

"Derek," he said. "Get the clutter out of your mind. Don't think about your hard home life, or the test you have to take tomorrow, or the fact that you don't have any money. Stay in the fight. Stay here now. If you don't take care of the 'now,' you're going to get your ass whipped!"

That was some of the best advice I have ever received. As soon as I applied it to martial arts, I became much better. I immediately realized that nothing can put clutter in your mind like a fight. But once I cleared my mind and learned to live in the now, everything slowed down for me on the mat and I found that I became so clear in my thinking that the matches seemed to move in slow motion. The struggle was gone.

After a few months of clear thinking on the judo mat, I noticed that the coach's advice had begun to carry over into other aspects of my life. Rather than ponder the past or fear the future, I began to live in the now. The words of my coach stayed with me in times of worry or personal conflict. "Stay in the fight. Stay here now. If you don't take care of the 'now,' you're going to get your ass whipped!" As I applied that advice to all aspects of my life – not just the battle on the mat – I noticed that the struggle subsided, and in many cases, stopped. No matter what the personal struggle was – family, school, my own demons – the struggle became easier or stopped altogether if I applied my coach's advice of staying here now. My mind became clear, events slowed down, breathing became easier, self-criticism diminished, self-worth increased; If I applied my coach's advice. If...

With just the simple discipline of thinking a thought, repeating it like a mantra, I could all but stop the struggle in my life.

I felt as though I was in the grace of a higher power.

Oddly enough, it was the power of living in the now that allowed me to delve even deeper into the notion of a higher power.

Let's jump forward a decade, and I'll tell you what I mean. And yes, it is okay to jump forward, backward, even sideways in this book because time is not linear. We jump around in our minds all the time, observing our life as though it is a range of mountains we can only appreciate visually, with no ability to change its shape. So, let's jump forward right now so I can illustrate how the power of now sensitized me to a higher power.

It was two years after the death of my mother, and I was in downtown Dublin with a colleague. I had graduated from my psychotherapy studies, and was in the midst of building a practice. Now, as a break from doing my weekend paperwork, I decided to attend a Mind, Body, Health exhibition. If you have never been to such an event, I can sum them up by saying they are convention center events with exhibits that are a crazy salad of all things related to health and wellness. And I mean all things. A booth where the health benefits of colon cleansing advocated by stark photos of tarry stools, can be found sandwiched between a vegamatic demonstration, and a tarot card reader. These exhibitions are massive, and I don't mean just in their physical scope. They are massive in that they represent every shape and form of thought that can be found about health, wellness, and the human spirit.

As a smart young psychotherapist with a fresh new qualification, I strolled around this exhibition with an air of superiority. Words like "bullshit" and "ill-logical" spilled from my mouth, as I commented on what I saw on either side of the aisles. In short, I was not living in the now.

Had I been living in the now, I would have suspended criticism by not involving the skepticism of my past, nor the critical faculties that had been pounded into me during my psychotherapy training. I would have observed, asked questions, listened, looked and weighed everything later when....

"Excuse me," said a gangly young man. "Would you like to have your aura photographed?"

"No effing way," I said, echoing the superiority that often comes with a new education. "That's all bull"....

"Sure, he wants one," said my colleague. "Get up there Derek. Live a little."

I sat where the young man pointed and smiled as the photo was taken. I hoped that none of my colleagues were around to see what I was doing.

Practitioners of aura photography believe that an energy field surrounds our body and can be captured using a special camera, its called Kirlian Photography. They believe this energy field reveals information about our physical and mental health, and can even contain information from influential people in our lives. When my photo was processed there were bright and beautiful colors around my head. I still have the photo. The bright color of light around my head reminds me of an Indian headdress, one of those spectacular crowns of brightly colored feathers that encircle the head and tumble down the back. In this photo these feathers are represented by full spectrum light emanating from my head, a phenomenon that looks as though a rainbow is emerging from my skull. The one irregularity in this photo is a red spot surrounded by an irregular black border. It stands out in sharp relief from the other colors surrounding it, and is right over my heart.

"Hmmm," said the man who took the photo, sounding like a radiologist who had just seen a tumor in an x-ray. "I am psychic and I'm getting a message from this photo. Do you mind if I tell you what it is?"

A few moments earlier I would have dismissed such talk and left the booth. But the spot stood out so much that I was now curious. "Sure," I said, and sat back down to hear the young stranger's message.

The young man looked at the photo and then at me.

"I have your mother here, her name is Agnes. She is sitting at a table with what looks like a glass of water." I was shocked for some reason.

"It's not water, it's vodka," I insisted, remembering very clearly her drink of choice.

"Okay, vodka," said the psychic, flatly. He was silent for a moment perhaps because he could see that I was starting to come undone. "She is telling me to tell you that she is very, very sorry about the argument the two of you had on her last day. She says you need to understand that if she knew she was going to die, that there was no way she would have said what she did."

I was stunned by what the psychic had said. My mind went back 10 years. I was in my twenties and caring for my mother. I had watched helplessly as alcohol completed its sinister goal of turning her from a lovely woman into a witch. The last year of her life had seen her world fall completely apart. She no longer took care of herself at all. Where she used to care about her appearance, she now didn't brush her hair all day. When I went to visit, I would most often find her at the kitchen table, sipping vodka from a glass, and staring into the void. She rarely changed out of her housecoat, and she became savagely angry when one of us children suggested that she might dress up and leave the house for some fresh air. In those last days, she preferred her life dark and lonely because it was how her mind had become. With every visit, I could tell that the booze and memories were making her more angry, and more crazy. With each passing day, she seemed to be looking for someone or something to blame for her plight. We all knew it would be just a short amount of time before she would focus her blame on me, or the other siblings who had taken on the unpleasant task of taking care of her, yet still we continued to care for her because there was no other way.

Every couple of days I would drop by her house with groceries, so her entire caloric intake wouldn't just be alcohol. But these were her final days – I know that now – and the vodka that she drank constantly had finally driven her mad.

The day the psychic was talking about came back to me clearly. I remembered walking into the living room and seeing my mother in the kitchen. She was breathing heavily and mumbling, as her gaze fixed on me through a haze of cigarette smoke. I knew I was in for some rough talk I just didn't know why.

"There was a can of salmon in the refrigerator yesterday and it's gone now," she growled, sounding more like a demon than a mother.

"I don't know anything about it," I said.

"You liar! You thief!" she shouted as she stood up and waved frantically toward the door. "Get the hell out of this house you fucking robber! You fucking thief!"

Her tirade continued as she insisted, I had stolen a can of salmon and she began to wonder out loud whether I had stolen anything else of value from her home. She stood so close to me and raged, that I could feel the heat of anger in her breath, and see in her eyes the delirium caused by years of drinking. At this horrible moment, I fell completely out of love with my mother.

"You venomous bitch," I said, backing toward the door. "I am fucking sick and tired of you drinking and ruining everybody else's life. I bring you groceries every day. How dare you accuse me of stealing."

As I opened the door to leave, I spoke the last words I would ever say to my mother.

"I hope you burn in hell!"

Later that evening she died.

The guilt associated with those final words rang in my ears. They stay with me still.

I was so ashamed by those final words that I had never

told anyone but my wife about that last exchange with my mother. Yet now the secret was revealed by a psychic stranger, right here in the middle of an exhibition hall where hundreds of people could see my reaction. At the time, I couldn't think. I kept saying, "Thank you, mom, I'm sorry too," but I couldn't see my mother, only the face of the slightly nervous psychic who had delivered the message from…. Where?

I began to tremble and then right there, in front of dozens of strangers, who were suddenly drawn to the drama in this aura photography booth, I began to weep. Uncontrollably. I remembered all too vividly the event the psychic was referring to. "Thank you," I said and then I said it again. "Thank you." I said it again, but I didn't know who I was thanking, the psychic for delivering the message, or my mom for saying it.

Later that day, I told my wife Linda the entire story. I was amazed at the power of the experience. Something I had only mildly believed in – that a person claiming to be psychic could accurately read the life of a stranger – had actually happened in a verifiable way. And, it had only happened because I had allowed an experience into my life that I would have ordinarily rejected. Now, that experience was going to affect not only me, but all of the people in my practice who were also searching for ways to stop the struggle of life. Through this one powerful psychic experience, I knew for certain that there was a higher power, an unseen force, that could lead to self-understanding. I had, suddenly and accidentally, found a tool of great value, both personally, and for my practice.

Over the years, I have realized that the higher power we are guided by is just that, it's a higher power, one that is truly out of our grasp, one that we reach for but never truly reach. Higher power has been defined in many ways. In its most general definition, higher power means a loving and caring power that is greater than the individual seeking the definition. This power doesn't have to be God, or anything that might be considered religious. In fact, in one study done by sociologist Darren Sherkat and based on 8,000 adults polled by the National Opinion Research Center, eight percent said that they did not believe in a personal God, yet "believe in a higher power of some kind."

To touch that higher power doesn't always involve psychic revelations, or other types of information that one might consider to be garnered from a spiritual realm, but it does always involve revelations. In fact, I tell my patients, that seeking a higher power involves revelations that make us more comfortable with ourselves and the world around us. They are also revelations that make us realize there is help out there, we just can't always see it. Some might call this Higher Power, God, or collective unconscious, or fate, or luck, or happenstance. What it's called doesn't matter. The acknowledgment that it exists, does. It's the acknowledgment that a Higher Power exists, that allows you to explore the experiences in your life for deeper personal meaning.

I could go on and on, but the essence of reaching one's higher power, is to live on a minute-by-minute basis, and to accept the experiences the universe gives you, without trying to filter them out. All experience is worthy of examination, even if it conflicts with your worldview. In fact, experience should be examined, especially if it conflicts with your worldview. In this book, we are trying to stop the struggle in our lives. And, it is generally a worldview we are trapped in, that keeps us from escaping the struggle. We must always seek in a fluid way to get closer to the truth, because without that quality of seeking, we become ossified in our beliefs, and never truly touch our higher power.

Hillary was one such patient who struggled with a need to be loved. There is nothing wrong with needing to be loved, we all have that need. But for Hillary, it was a toxic need, one that led her to a chain of short-term boyfriends who didn't have the same need for her as she did for them. Hillary was tired of this sort of life and decided she needed help, which is how she found herself in my office.

"I am struggling with love," she told me in a bemused way. "It seems as though I only give it and never get it. Oh sure, men tell me they love me but not for long. I am the girl they pass through on their way to a more permanent relationship."

Hillary was no girl. She was nearly 40 years old and had never had a satisfying long-term relationship with a man. She said it was time to change her life, and I agreed.

I told her that the struggle for love was one of mankind's main struggles, and that I had techniques and tools that could change her life, if she used them. But first, she had to master self-love, and be willing to reach out to her Higher Power.

Hillary sneered at the notion of a higher power, and then at me.

"I'm not religious," she said. "There has to be a different way to get over my issues than prayer."

"I'm not talking about prayer," I said. "I'm talking about a higher power. There are a lot of ways to look at the notion of a higher power. For most people, it's God. But for others, it's just the force that animates us and makes us alive. Some people believe that higher power is just motivation for personal growth. If you look at it that way, maybe the idea of a higher power is just what fuels growth and change, like water does to a plant."

She didn't totally buy the notion of a higher power, nor its importance to personal change, but she said she was willing to try anything to get over her struggles with love.

I gave her the techniques outlined at the end of this chapter, and asked her to follow them at least twice a day. "It'll be easier than prayer," I joked. After all, everything is just energy coming and going, but how we spend that energy, and with whom is really important.

A week later, I met with a "newer" Hillary, one who had not only a sense of the higher power I had been talking about, but its role in clearing up her issues.

"I am realizing that not all of our decisions are made consciously, that there are forces in the universe that can help us in ways that we don't fully understand," she said. "And we have to trust those forces/energy."

Lesson: Reaching Your Higher Power

I have found that higher power is best reached through the element of intuition, which is the state of knowing something instinctively without having to discover or perceive it. Some people consider intuition to be divine guidance, while others might think of it as a connection to collective unconscious, or others just our fabulous brain at work. I don't think it matters how one sees its ultimate origin, just that they realize it exists and are willing to access it.

For me, intuition can at times seem to be almost supernatural, like cases where a person makes a snap decision to not take a particular airplane flight, and it crashes. But intuition is usually more benign, and is subconsciously involved in almost every decision we make. If you have ever thought, "I don't know why I made that decision but it was the right one," or "Something told me I shouldn't do that, but I did it anyway," then you have seen intuition in action. Every time I have followed that invisible voice called, intuition, it has been the right thing to do. Whether it was feelings I followed about not taking drugs with my friends when I was young, or deciding at the spur of the moment to combine Eastern ways of thought with Western psychology, or even having my aura photographed, my intuition has always been my best guide. When Princeton historian Joseph Campbell advised his students to, "Follow your bliss," he was certainly referring to intuition, or another way of saying it, is gut feeling.

There are ways to put your intuition, your higher power, at your fingertips.

Look back at your past for the very last time

And I mean, "the last time." Don't keep revisiting it, or you will be caught in a loop. There are people who spend decades in psychotherapy because they are trapped by negative pivot points and do nothing but relive the past. The best way to move beyond unpleasant events from the past, is to attempt to forget them and move beyond them. Forgiving is good, forgetting is better.

Now look back at your past again, one more time

Now look back at your past again, focusing on all that's negative in your life. Bring these issues to the front of your mind and look at them clearly. As you do this, let the emotions you experience wash over you, and hold nothing back as you respond to them. Now take the past out of your life. Try not to think about it anymore (you'll be surprised how easy this is) and especially stop talking about it. Why? Because talking about negative events amplifies them, keeping them large in your mind. Let them go and they shrink over time. Let them shrink. You can't do anything about the past, so why dwell on it?

Take a look around you

Focus on now. Take a look around you. Look at the color of the walls, the art hung on them, the height of the ceiling, the colors in the art, the people walking by the window. Don't think about the past, or the future, (they don't truly exist anyway) just focus on the now. Keep focusing on the now. Do you feel a weight lift from your body? Ask yourself: Where am I? Then ask yourself: Who am I? Then the big question: Who's asking? Try this answer to any question you have about existence. Soon your thoughts will turn inward, and your focus will change to the immediate, that knife's edge of time we all live on.

Move toward your higher power

By living in the now you are free of the weight of the past and the uncertainty of the future. Enjoying the sense of freedom and energy? Congratulations, you have just connected with your higher power.

Of course, these four steps to your higher self sound easy, and they are. It's the execution that is difficult. Living in the now requires constant adjustment in your thinking. It calls for you to erase events of the past from your mind, and to avoid negative thoughts of the future. It calls for you to live in that moment called *The Now*, the only reality that truly exists.

Had I not been reminded to live in the now by my colleague at the exhibition hall, I would not have had the psychic reading that turned out to be a pivotal experience in my life. Instead, I would have passed the booth, and with it the chance to be introduced to my higher self.

As a result of this experience, I became a student of *The Now*, and stayed on the path to my higher power. This is a path that many have chosen throughout history, regardless of their religious or spiritual leanings, or even if they have them at all.

Without learning how to live in *The Now*, I would never have truly understood the quotations:

> "I have realized that the past and future are
> real illusions, that they exist in the present,
> which is what there is and all there is."
> -Alan Watts

"Finish each day and be done with it. You have done what you could; some blunders and absurdities have crept in; forget them as soon as you can. Tomorrow is a new day; you shall begin it serenely and with too high a spirit to be encumbered with your old nonsense."

\- Ralph Waldo Emerson

Questions and Answers

Question: I'm still not sure I understand: Why does *living in the now* lead to contact with our higher self?

Answer: By living in a *clocked second*, in other words, by living as close to the actual time as possible, what happens is the conscious and unconscious mind are two separate parts…and the unconscious mind has no reference point for time. If you retrieve a memory that is 20 years old, it is actually stored, at the exact same level, as a memory that happened only 10 seconds ago.

The unconscious mind has no reference point for time, and yet the unconscious mind is where the higher self resides. Your higher self is the all-knowing, the wise one, because it has laid out in front of it, every single event that has ever happened to you. It knows the cause of the event, and it knows how to stop the event, and that's why it's important to live by what we call *The Now* or a *clocked second*. That's when the higher self can come forward and give you the answers, and at times, the profound answers, to questions that you've always been looking for the answers to.

Question: Is there something about living in the now that can make us more psychic?

Answer: Well, the fact of the matter is, that the word psychic has been abused, it's actually more about being intuitive. And, by being intuitive, it means being present, fully being there, right at that moment in time. By doing that, you become more intuitive. You get a gut feeling about somebody or someplace. You get a gut feeling that this is a safe place, or this is a good guy, or this deal is honest. There's nothing psychic about that. It's just a matter of being right here, right now, making a valued judgment and using all your senses. Intuition is part of the survival mechanism that's built into us. Usually the quieter we are, the more powerfully intuitive we become, and the more positive the outcomes we will have to our actions.

Question: What effect does living in the now have on anxiety?

Answer: If you live in the now, there is no past, no future, and no event taking place. If you look at it that way, you don't worry about the past (because it's gone), nor about the future (because it hasn't arrived). Because of that, it gets rid of anxiety. Most people will run themselves to death with anxiety, by thinking about future events that, actually, never happen. So, that's why, by learning to stay present with yourself, you'll find that anxiety disappears.

Question: How is it that living in the now will make one more perceptive?

Answer: By living in the now, you are living like a baby because you see things fresh. Your mind is clear because it's not thinking about the past, nor is it projecting a possible future. It is right in the now and dealing with everything happening in this moment. That makes events clearer and more truthful. You can see them, feel them, experience them anew. In doing so, you're achieving the access to the perceptive tools that are in your psyche, ones that can be used to help you with the situation that has developed in the moment.

Question: Does living in the now mean that we have to forget the past?

Answer: No. You don't have to forget the past. What you can do, is put the past to rest, or integrate it. How you do this is to make a pact with yourself that you will pay attention to the past, just to see if there's anything there to be dealt with. When you have dealt with the past, it is then put to rest. There may be issues that come back, but remember, the past is truly something you cannot change. It's a waste of energy to be looking at it for any other reason, except to deal with the positive stuff you want to manifest. All of this can be achieved with a few deep breaths to bring you into the Now.

CHAPTER 4

Reaching Higher

"Until you make the unconscious conscious, it
will direct your life and you will call it fate."
Carl Jung

The accurate reading from the psychic left me stunned. The final communication with my mother was a private wound that I carried with me in silence. I was ashamed of the final exchange I had with my mother, and as a result had told no one but my wife about it. But now a perfect stranger had "read it" in an aura photograph. What was that about? I realized I had been touched by a higher power, but I didn't know exactly what that meant. All I truly knew was a feeling of extreme relief, as a weight of sorrow and guilt was lifted from my shoulders.

Though I had been having these sorts of experiences my whole life, this was yet another confirmation. Most obvious to me was the nature of the psychotherapy profession. In my estimation, there was nothing better than knowing oneself, and no better way to do that than by probing one's own psyche. But now, I began to doubt that the psychotherapy profession allowed patients to go far enough.

I began to look for anything in my life that compared to the experience of the aura photograph. What I remembered were incidents that took place when I was studying hypnotherapy at psychotherapy school, where we students hypnotized one another to improve technique and ability.

I was a natural born hypnotist. Within a few minutes, I could put a fellow student into a state of deep hypnosis and reach deep into their psyche. Sometimes I reached too deep. Some of the students I hypnotized reported that they were going into past lives, seeing themselves as people who lived years – even centuries – ago. It was typical to hear stories from students who transformed into ancient Greeks, medieval farmers, young students from the 19th century, and so forth, during the course of, their hypnosis sessions. They were puzzled at where they had gone and what they had learned during our sessions, and wanted to know what had happened.

The same thing happened to me. I asked a fellow student to hypnotize me, and when he took me deep into the process, he told me to remember the last day of my last life. I had a vivid memory of being a Buddhist monk, a memory that surprised me greatly since I had never given two thoughts to Buddhism.

What were these past lives about?

Surely, my instructor had encountered past lives before? He had, after all, taught hypnotherapy for at least two decades. Someone in the thousands of patients he had treated must have experienced something they considered to be a past life. I made an appointment with him one afternoon and told him what had happened during these hypnotherapy sessions. He pretended to listen patiently, but I could tell that he had no patience for what I was saying. He admitted that he too had encountered past lives during hypnosis sessions, but felt they were nothing more than "false memory." I think this was because of his strong Catholic upbringing.

"People want to have lived in a past life, so they wish it on themselves," he said. "They imagine stories about themselves, and when they are hypnotized these stories come out like very vivid dreams. Yet they are just wish fulfillment."

I didn't argue because I didn't want to do anything that might jeopardize my grades. But, I didn't believe his explanation either. I had never thought about Buddhist monks, let alone wished to be one, and the students I hypnotized had never wished to be the individuals they had become during hypnosis. Although it was clear that the professor had encountered past lives in his patients many times, I felt that he had come at the subject with preconceived notions. He had never explored the facts of the stories told to him by the puzzled patients, nor had he ever told them to do any more than doubt their experience. He had no interest in exploring these curiosities, and furthermore, made it clear that I should have no interest in exploring them, either.

He called past life experiences "factoids", which he defined as something that may not be true but is accepted as truth because it is often repeated.

"But if it's often repeated, that means it happens often during hypnosis," I said. "Shouldn't we at least explore them to see where they go?"

The frown on his face told me I had crossed a line that took him out of his comfort zone. I thanked him for his answer and never introduced questions about past lives again.

After the encounter with my professor, I decided to ignore past lives. And later, when I was in private practice, I decided to ignore them too, believing against belief that the spontaneous past life regressions that took place with my patients, were simply false memory as my instructor had insisted.

But now, the event with the aura photo had changed my attitude. I knew this strange event had allowed me to experience a higher power. I began to realize that the "unseen world" extended beyond the "psyche," and "subconscious," and the other standards of psychotherapy school. For me it clearly extended into such arenas as "psychic" and "past lives." I wanted to study more of it. And I knew my patients would want more of it, too.

I decided to change the way I did analysis.

Up until now, I had focused on the mechanics of psychotherapy, even becoming a supervisor with my association to train other therapists how to stay between the lines. I asked all of the right questions - the textbook questions - and then asking another question, when the patient made a brief pause that may not have signified the true end of their answer. Now I made a conscious effort to focus on the art of psychotherapy, an approach that consisted of letting the patient sit in silence after their response, pushing the patient with this uncomfortable silence to fill the void with deeper thoughts about their interior world.

This simple technique alone allowed my patients to have astounding breakthroughs in their issues. And, some of the ones who went beyond ordinary talk therapy and on to hypnotherapy, began to explore – much to their surprise – past lives. A patient who was a musical prodigy at age five, found himself living in 17th century Munich as a member of an orchestra. A woman with a string of failed marriages, found herself a courtesan in 16th century France…and so on. Patients were suddenly getting answers to their psychological problems that had evaded them for years.

Were these patients truly going back into past lives? That was for them to decide. For me it was satisfaction enough, that a change in technique led to rapid improvement.

There were, however, mysteries.

One such mystery was a teenage boy who came to me to overcome a stammer. I hypnotized him hoping to find an event in his childhood, a trauma perhaps, that may have caused this speech impediment. In the beginning of the session he recalled very normal childhood memories, affectionate visits with his grandparents, rough-housing with pets, and kicking a soccer ball to his father. Then, in the midst of the ordinary, he said, "That's funny, the person I am isn't me."

I convinced him to continue, telling him that it was my job to analyze what he was seeing, no matter how strange. With that, the young man described himself as wearing a black, blousy tunic, and standing before a large mansion where he had "lived and died."

As the session progressed, the young man described his life in the mansion as being one of misery. "My relationship with my parents is bad," he said, switching into the present tense. "They give all of their attention to my sister and treat me as though I am in the way."

As the session continued, the young man became more and more angry about his situation. No one in the house seemed to love him. Rather, his parents lavished all of their affections on his sister, and rarely acknowledged his existence. Out of jealousy and rage, the young man finally made a horrible decision, he was going to murder his sister.

The years of this past life were before electricity, when it was common to have a candle burning all night, so a room wouldn't be in total darkness. Sitting before me in his hypnotic state, the young man recalled how he had snuck into his sister's bedroom late at night when she was asleep, and lit her curtain on fire with one of these candles. His plan was to make her death look like an accident, but the curtain caught fire much more rapidly than he expected, and he found himself trapped in the room by a wall of flame. Gasping for breath during the session, he described how the room was now filling with smoke. He described his feelings of being trapped, and even began to call for help during the session. Then, as he described the heat and smoke, he seemed to give up like a person who was overwhelmed by circumstances. Then his consciousness seemed to pull back as though he had left his body. He talked about collapsing to the floor and feeling intense heat.

"I'm so sorry," he said, beginning to weep. "I'm so sorry."

He sobbed for a few moments and then fell silent, as though he had relived his own death. He remembered the experience vividly after the session was over, and stayed in the chair for some time, shaking his head, and wiping his eyes.

Despite the trauma of this memory, it presented the root cause of his stammer. He left the office that day, unaware that his stammer had disappeared. It was on his return for his next session, that he entered with great delight that he had barely stammered during the week, and now was talking perfectly fine. I told him we need not do any more work and released him from therapy.

I paid careful attention to what the young man said in this and subsequent sessions, and took copious notes about the specifics of his past life description. He not only presented the approximate dates of the event, but also his name in his past life.

What is the chance that an 18 year old would know anything about a fire taking place in a house in 1806, I asked myself. I went to a librarian in Dublin and asked if he knew of any suspicious house fires in manors around this time. He said he would look into it, and within a few weeks he told me about the nobles who owned the land currently known as "Clondalkin Valley." It was there that the McManus family tragically lost their two children to a fire that had been described as an accident, one in which the youngsters burned to death when a candle in a bedroom caught the curtains on fire.

Based on what I had heard from my patient, there was little question in my mind that the fire had been caused by my jealous patient in his past life. There was also little question that by living the final experiences of his past life, and bringing this painful experience forward through future sessions, that he had been cured of his stammer.

The young man's experience had opened this new world for me a little more. I was clearly moving toward a higher power, and with it more knowledge about what it is and how it's perceived. I realized that talking about a higher power is almost meaningless. The only way a higher power can be described is by experiencing it. This presents a problem to the world of science, because the notion of a higher force is not a reproducible phenomenon, and therefore can't be looked at scientifically. Yet it's there, as much a part of our inner world as our subconscious mind, which can also be the subject of some skepticism by the scientific community.

I had no interest in rejecting the scientific community, but I realized I had moved outside of it. I was experiencing something that only I could truly experience. What had happened up until this point was my own spiritual reality, and I was really the only one who could assess the meaning and power of that.

It wasn't long until this new world opened a little more.

For years I had been having an inconceivable dream, one that didn't fit into my cultural upbringing at all. In this dream, I found myself sitting very still in a cave. I could see myself, and what I saw horrified me. It looked as though I had been sitting very still for years. I was so dirty

I looked as though I was rotting. My teeth were changing color and literally dropping out of my head, and my hair had grown beyond my waist. I was emaciated and could feel rats and other tiny animals biting my skin. Still, I remained so disciplined that I didn't move, even though the bites, and dirty skin, created powerful itches that I did not scratch. On top of all of this, there was dark green ivy growing all over me, so much so that I looked like a living pile of leaves.

Although this dream took place regularly, it never lasted long enough for me to find out why I was in this cave in the first place. Was I a convict who had gone insane? Was I a stroke victim unable to move? Was I a seeker, searching for the meaning of life? I speculated as to why I was there, but in truth, I had no idea.

For the longest time, I thought this was just a dream. Then one day I heard about a psychic from Australia whose specialty was past life readings. I read about her first in the newspaper. Then there was a radio interview in which she confidently declared that we have multiple lives. "Memory of these lives are contained in our brain, and all we need to do is unlock them," she insisted. She advocated hypnosis as the most effective way to explore these lives, but said she didn't need to use it. She was psychic, she said, and could reach a person's past lives through her psychic powers.

I decided to visit her.

I went to the office where she was taking appointments and introduced myself. I didn't tell her I was a psychotherapist and hypnotherapist, I just gave her my name.

She didn't seem to care who I was, or what I did, anyway. She had me sit across a small breakfast table from her and then she just sat still, looking like she was tuning into something only she could hear.

"Strange," she said after several minutes. "I'm seeing you in a cave. You are deep in meditation, but you look sick. You are covered with leaves. . ."

She went on for sometime describing my appearance in the cave, even estimating the temperature around me ("It's so hot that you are longing for a breeze."), and the view I was looking at ("There are snow-capped peaks in the distance, but in front of them is a mountain village that keeps distracting you."), even some of the tiny critters that would race into the cave and nibble at my body. I was so still they must have thought I was dead.

My heart began to race as she told me what she was seeing. It was my dream to a tee! But what else did she know? With her visual description being so accurate, I asked if she had any idea why I was there.

"Certainly," she said, maintaining that faraway gaze. "You have a job to do. Your whole task is to hold a psychic consciousness to alleviate suffering in the world. In this life, you are a monk, and your job is to pray away evil."

I felt my consciousness take a leap forward. For years I had felt that this was just a bad dream, one that lingered for reasons I could not figure out. At times, I even thought it was a sign of some kind of mental imbalance. But now, sitting across from a stranger who knew the dream and its meaning, and who believed it was not a dream at all but a past life, I felt as though I had taken another giant step toward a higher power.

A number of fears died for me that day. I no longer feared death. I no longer even thought it took place. After the last several experiences I had – from the aura photo with my mother's message, to the past lives of patients, and then my own – the possibility of complete obliteration of our consciousness didn't seem remotely possible.

Any doubt I had about my intuition, also died that day. I saw intuition as a means of guidance that takes place on an unconscious level. Rather than question those guiding feelings, I decided to trust them and not rationalize them until they disappeared. This was also the day that my views of organized religion changed. I did not reject the religion of my birth – I identify myself as a Catholic and always will – but I felt I had discovered a spiritual world that had never been presented to me before, and I couldn't ignore it. It was as though I had discovered a religion inside of myself, one that contained the elements of fearless death, karma, and a memory that lives on and continues to influence us forever.

More than ever, I believed in something I have already said in this book, that we have bought the ticket to life, but we are only watching half the show. I was now convinced that a deeper memory contained information about our many lives. Why this memory isn't readily available to us, I don't know, but I was sure that by working at it we could reach this memory, and continue to improve as human beings, through the lessons of our past lives. Needless to say, I wanted to see more.

I decided to trust my intuition and take some formal training in Eastern philosophy. Rather than jump right into the *Bhagavad Gita* or the *Tibetan Book of the Dead*, I thought it would be best to study the thoughts and work of Carl Jung, the Swiss psychologist who founded analytical psychology and believed that the human psyche is inherently religious. Jung studied Christianity, Hinduism, Buddhism, Gnosticism and Taoism, and concluded that at the heart of all religions are thoughts and images that are shared by all people, a collective unconscious, that is responsible for what we become as individuals. This "individuation" is at the center of all religions, and is part of our search for self and the Divine. "So powerful is spirituality," wrote Jung, "it should be used as a cure for alcoholism." This is some of the smart advice that helped create the foundation of Alcoholics Anonymous.

Jung's interest in all things deep in the psyche – including religion, the occult, dream interpretation, mysticism – led him to personally induce hallucinations – a form of meditation called "active imagination". Jung meditated to reach a state of active imagination, which allowed him to communicate with the conscious and unconscious aspects of his psyche, in essence his higher power.

If all of this sounds a bit heady, it is. But perhaps he summed up his feeling about intuition and self-exploration when he said, "Your vision will become clear only when you can look into your own heart. Who looks outside, dreams; who looks inside, awakes."

My formal training in psychotherapy had ignored Jung's more spiritual path in favor of Freud's far less spiritual approach. With my recent experiences, I felt a need to study therapy that included a heavy dose of Eastern philosophy, and offered techniques to reach one's higher power. I chose to enroll in an advanced course on the work of Carl Jung. And that was when a coincidence happened that led me in an entirely different direction.

I was in Dun Laoghaire, a seaside resort near Dublin, with my wife and daughter. We were there for a day's outing when I found myself wandering the streets looking for an activity more intellectual than sunbathing. I soon found myself in a bookstore perusing the psychology section in search of books by Carl Jung, particularly a book with the dry title of *The Pathology of Everyday Life*. I found the book high on a shelf, and as I pulled it down another book from a lower shelf fell and hit me on the foot.

As I bent to pick up the fallen book, my daughter approached and stuck a box of incense sticks into my face. "Daddy, I bought you these," she said, putting the bundle of sticks into my hands. I read the label. There was a picture of a bushy haired man dressed in orange with words that introduced him as "Sathya Sai Baba."

I held the incense sticks in one hand and then picked up the book. For a moment I thought my brain had confused it with the incense. The title was, *Sai Baba, Man of Miracles*. I was holding a book and incense with the name of Sai Baba on them. Something magical had clearly happened. I bought the book immediately and left the bookstore.

That night I went to my office, which was a room in my house, after the kids were put to bed, and began to read the book. As I read it, I could feel the hairs on my neck rise and tingle with anger. In this book, they were saying that

98

Sai Baba was capable of performing the same miracles as Jesus. Is this guy some kind of Antichrist, I thought as I pinched the book shut, and threw it into the trash bin.

I thought nothing more of the book until the next morning. I had a full day of appointments to look forward to and no time to think of an Indian madman with a Jesus complex. I went into my office and waited for the first patient to arrive. Instead, I received a telephone call from the apologetic patient who said she had to stay home to care for her son because he had become ill and had to stay home from school. We rescheduled, and then I received another phone call and another, all patients canceling their appointments. Within an hour, seven patients had cancelled, and I suddenly found myself with a free day. Such a thing had never happened to me before, nor since.

I eyed the book in the trash bin and decided to give it one more chance. Once again, I felt anger and anxiety as I read the book about Sathya Sai Baba.

Born in 1926 as Sathyanarayana Raju in India, Sathya Sai Baba seemed to be a normal and average citizen of Puttaparthi in central India. In 1940 all that changed, when the young man was bitten by a scorpion while visiting his brother in the nearby town of Uravakonda. For several hours young Baba became unconscious, when he awoke, he seemed almost other-worldly. He began to laugh and weep, and had periods of great eloquence followed by silence. He began to sing Sanskrit verses, even though he had no prior knowledge of the language.

Sathya's parents brought their son back to Puttaparthi, where they took him to a variety of medical doctors, priests and exorcists. Nothing changed. Sathya remained, as one doctor called him, "Hysterical."

In May of 1940, Sathya called his family and friends together and materialized manna and flowers from thin air. All were shocked at what they saw, especially Sathya's father, who began to beat his son with a stick to get the devils out of him. With stick in hand, Sathya's father demanded to know who his son really was, to which Sathya replied that he was "Sai Baba of Shirdi," a 19th-century saint who had died eight years before Sathya was born.

After that proclamation, Sathya became a guru, and yes, a miracle maker. He founded an ashram that drew millions from around the world, and then began his true mission, which included social welfare and charity work.

His fundraising abilities were amazing and were largely propelled by his wisdom, magic, and purported healing abilities. He raised enough money to complete an ashram called Prasanthi Nilayam in 1948, and then established a General Hospital in Puttaparthi. Later in his life, he went on to establish a free specialty hospital in Bangalore, and initiated a clean water project that eventually succeeded in providing drinking water to 1.2 million people. His charitable works support projects in 166 countries, and Sai Educare schools in 33 countries. He even went so far as to create three free universities for men and women, and an institute for Indian classical music.

It certainly wasn't his charity work that repelled me. Indeed, the Government of India released a postage stamp of Sai Baba honoring his work in safe drinking water. Rather it was his supposed miracles. They seemed completely outrageous.

Sai Baba said he performed miracles to attract people, which allowed him to transform them spiritually. His most common miracles were the materialization of vibhuti, a "holy ash" that appeared at the ends of his fingertips. But he also materialized photos of himself, bracelets, rings, watches – he seemed to be a veritable jewelry store for mystical objects. But Sai Baba's miracles transcended trinkets. Many claimed he was able to heal the sick and even raise the dead. At one point, he claimed to have healed himself of a stroke and four heart attacks publicly in front of thousands of people.

"Magic can have life-transforming effects on devotees," I read in the book. "The miraculous is absolutely central to this religious movement."

As I read the book, I became enamored of his charity work. I was becoming interested in helping the underprivileged, and the shear amount of successful charity work he managed to do captivated me. In fact, I felt that to do as much charity work as he had was supernatural, in itself. Just think of the supernatural amount of drive and charisma it would take to raise enough funds to build such an empire of charity. By some estimates, the Sathya Sai Organization has spent as much as $31 billion on dozens of charitable ventures worldwide.

But was he the supernatural healer he claimed? I had my doubts. To go from being a scorpion-bit youth to an astounding healer in the mold of Jesus seemed very far-fetched. I flipped through the book one more time and threw it in the garbage again, this time for good. But as I sat in silence, I heard a very clear voice in my head say, "Why don't you write me?" This was clearly an Indian voice, not the voice I would normally hear, which was my own.

With nothing else to do, I reached in my desk drawer and pulled out a piece of stationary. The letter I wrote was simple. "My name is Derek. If you are who you and others say you are, send me vibhuti, and I will come."

I put the letter into an envelope and wrote the only address I knew: Sai Baba. India. I then rang a colleague and jokingly said, "I just wrote to God. He lives in India and looks like a mixture of Michael Jackson and Jimi Hendrix. So, make sure that they keep a comfortable padded room for me when the organization finds out", and we laughed together.

When I came back from the mailbox, my wife Linda was standing at the door to my office. "I just posted a letter to God", I said, laughing, "Or at least to someone who thinks he is."

I had violated the first rule of reaching out to your higher power: stay open to the possibilities. By writing the letter, I was mocking Sathya Sai Baba. I would soon learn my lesson.

Are you Derek O'Neill?

It was three months later, and I was attending another Mind/Body exhibition in Kildare. I had forgotten all about the letter I wrote to Sai Baba. I was passing through the hallways in a meditative state, looking and not thinking, letting the world pass by me and through me when I felt a tap on my shoulder.

"Are you Derek O'Neill?"

"I am," I said. "Do I know you?"

"You know of me," he said mysteriously. "Can I speak to you a moment?"

He led me to a table where we sat down and began to talk. My colleague I had rang about the padded room, happened to be there with me. So, I signaled for her to come to the table with me. He was an Irish guy wearing an orange shirt, and he just began to talk. He had a pleasantness about him. He did not introduce himself. Rather he began to introduce me to myself, talking as though he had known me for years and was just catching up. He knew about my mother and father and my siblings, and about the dynamics between us all. He knew about my wife and children, and knew absolutely everything about me, times, dates, and ages of events.

"I have something for you," he said, reaching into a satchel bag, he pulled out a tin about one and a half inches round, and in its center was a symbol that consisted of the symbols of the five major religions – Christianity, Islam, Hinduism, Buddhism, and Judaism. He pushed the tin across the table to me.

"You asked for vibhuti," he said, tapping the top of the tin. "Now you must come." I went into complete fear. Who was this guy? How did he know so much about me? I wanted to run away.

Fear gripped me, followed by happiness, then sadness, then anger, then love... I had learned in therapy class that you can hold only one emotion at a time, and that was the case here. Emotions rolled through me one at a time, as I reached for the tin and pulled it close to me. I opened it and saw the powdery substance, and knew that what had happened to me was a moment of magic, and I knew that this moment would have a transformative effect on me, yet the fear overwhelmed me. Grabbing the tin, I said the words, "I can't talk to you anymore." As I stood to leave, my colleague who was standing next to us listening to the whole interaction, had turned to walk away with me but walked into the wall. Grabbing her by the arm, we ran out together.

We made our way to a café; she could see I was shaken and asked if I wanted a cup of coffee. I immediately said yes, although I had never had a cup of coffee in my life. When she handed me the coffee, I was shaking so much I spilled half of it. She was as pale and shaken as I was.

I felt like I was in a corner, one with no escape. At that point, I did what everyone else does; I began to deny what had happened, rationalize it away, picking it apart and discarding the pieces as only a psychotherapist can do. Just as I had almost convinced myself that the meeting was nothing more than a parlor trick, the door of the café opened, and an elegant Indian woman walked in wearing a green sari. This was still old Ireland, and it was very rare to see a woman in a sari. On this particular day, her presence froze both my companion and I.

The woman smiled beautifully at me and walked toward our table. I was horrified.

"Excuse me," she said, "but haven't I just seen you sitting with Sai Baba at the Mind/Body expo? You are very lucky. He is a great man."

We practically ran from the café. I didn't know Sai Baba yet, but I knew what he looked like, and the man who spoke to me looked nothing like the guru. Had she seen a manifestation of Sai Baba? Is it possible she didn't know what he looked like? Is it possible she was part of an elaborate hoax? My mind went in several different directions as my colleague drove me home, but it always arrived back at the same spot: something magical had happened.

I went in the house and told Linda what had happened. She listened calmly as I described what had happened and then issued a measured response.

"Well, you did ask for it, didn't you?"

Two weeks later, I booked a flight for India. Linda could not come, but the colleague who had been with me insisted on coming with me.

Lesson: All Is Not Known

Looking back on this chapter, I see an overriding message: All is not known. Some in science may pretend to know everything, but they don't. In fact, the truly honest ones in science admit that they don't know everything, and will even go so far as to say that all is not knowable. As Woody Allen so quizzically put it, "Is knowledge knowable? If not, how do we know?"

Don't be intimidated by the unknown, or those who criticize you for being curious about it. Fear of criticism leads to paralysis, while following your curious instincts will lead you to explore new paths, ones that can make you a new and better person with seemingly endless possibilities.

Questions & Answers

Question: Much of this chapter deals with past life regressions. Yet there are many people who don't believe in past lives. Do you think a past life experienced during hypnotherapy can be anything other than a past life?

Answer: It is not important whether somebody believes in a past life or not; their mind believes it and therefore, the healing comes from its belief. The other aspect of this question is, you can have all sorts of things like false memory syndrome, or cryptomnesia, where you may have read a book, or seen a movie in the distant past, that remains captured in your mind. These, too, can be part of a past life recall.

Question: Whether one believes in past lives or not, what are we supposed to do with the information we receive from a past life regression?

Answer: Past life regressions are based on the theory that what the mind sees, it believes, and this belief changes the mind to a positive or a negative. Past life regression can change one's perspective to be positive or negative, depending upon how an individual uses the information.

Question: In one of your past life experiences you were sitting in a cave and slowly rotting while tiny animals devoured you nibble by nibble. If this were a dream, what would it mean?

Answer: Well, if it was a dream, it would be telling me that there were aspects of my past that were nibbling away at me.

Question: Okay, maybe past life experiences aren't dreams, but are real. Where is the memory of our past lives stored? In our cells? Or is it memory that resides outside of our brain?

Answer: To begin with, past life experiences are not dreams. Memories of past lives are stored in the subconscious mind and then in turn, stored in our cells. That is why our subconscious minds can affect our physical state. This is why people can have past life experiences when they are receiving massages, and other forms of bodywork. Cellular memory can be activated by a touch, rub, or anger.

Question: In this chapter, you say that psychotherapist Carl Jung practiced "active imagination," a path to communicating with his "higher power." How does one practice active imagination?

Answer: Active Imagination is where you would actually sit down and ask yourself a specific set of questions. For example, one who feels they are in an abusive relationship might ask a simple series of questions like these:

- What do I find in this abusive relationship that is appealing to me?
- What was my life like before this relationship began?
- Is there anything in my upbringing that has led me to this kind of relationship?
- What would a relationship without abuse feel like?
- Does a relationship with abuse feel like peace and freedom, or does there seem to be something missing?

Once you ask these (or other) questions, take note of the pictures, feelings, thoughts, or experiences you have. It's a form of meditation, that has a spiritual and practical benefit.

CHAPTER 5

Great Expectations

"Never idealize others. They will never live up
to your expectations. A growing relationship
can only be nurtured by genuineness."
Leo Buscaglia

I knew nothing at all about the country and the people of India. It wasn't until the airplane began its descent over Madras, and we were at maybe 10,000 feet, that I realized that India was a country like no other. The heat began to build as the sun streamed through the tiny windows of the Air India flight. The pilot turned the air conditioning lower, but the heat from the rapidly setting sun fought it back, as we made our way to the ground. It was twilight as we were cleared to land, and our speeding plane seemed way too low to the ground on its approach to the airport. Below, I could see shanty towns peppered with cooking fires, that seemed to be just a few feet from the wheels of our aircraft. We were so close to the ground, that I could almost see detail in the richly colorful clothing of the women in the streets. No one down there looked up, which was comforting. In Western countries an approach this low would cause panic in the streets. But here, on the rim of an airport that handles more than 11 million travelers per year, I realized that the people in these wood and tin homes witness low approaches hundreds of times each week.

Still, there was the illusion of disaster. Just as I thought we were going to touch down on top of a town, the roofs passed under us and we thumped down on the tarmac. When we rolled to the gate and the door opened, India swept into the cabin and overwhelmed the plane with the furnace-like heat that hung oppressively outside. Within seconds the cabin smelled like cooking fires, incense, human shit, and dust. It was a smell that was new to me but was not wholly unpleasant. It was the smell of India.

At this point in my life, I had been out of Ireland only once, and that was to Spain with my wife for our honeymoon. There, the airports are clean and well organized. Now, my passport had been stamped at customs, and I was dragging my suitcase through a dirty airport, looking down a long hallway and out the glass doors ahead at what seemed to be a million people, many of whom were grabbing at the bags of tourists in hopes of coaxing them into badly dented cars that would leave immediately for hotels of questionable quality. It was a thrilling yet frightening scene all at the same time, and as I got closer to the mayhem, I wasn't sure if I should embrace it or run the other way.

I kept walking.

Outside, a haze of black flies flew wildly around my head. I swept my hand in front of my face, to ward them off, but the buzzing cloud stayed. On the ground below me were legless beggars sliding toward me through the sand, the palms of their dirty hands opened wide, their faces a picture of pity. I looked the other way, and was soon facing a broken man on crutches who held his face close to mine, his hand against my shirt begging for money. I looked the other way, a desperately dirty woman with a hungry child was closing in on me. I turned another way and saw what I thought were children playing in the sand because I could only see parts of their body. I was later to discover that these were deliberately amputated children used for begging to pull deeply on the heartstrings of foreigners and upper-class Indians.

"Let me help you," said an Indian man I had spoken to on the airplane. He took me by the arm to a cab and directed the driver to a hotel. In our conversation on the airplane, he had revealed that he was an electrical engineer for a large company in the United Kingdom and was returning home for his annual visit. I relaxed when he gave the driver the name of a hotel and shut the passenger door. Most likely he had become accustomed to Western comforts and would direct the driver to a hotel befitting an Irishman. I expected clean sheets and a warm shower and dreamed of those amenities as we wove through the bustling streets of Madras. My expectations were wrong. The room I found myself in had a hole in the floor for a toilet, a bucket for a shower, and a tarp for a shower curtain. By two a.m., I was in bed with the lights out, listening to street noise that never stopped and fighting bedbugs that felt like pricks from needles as they bit my legs. All I could do that night was wonder exactly why I had taken such a trip so far out of my comfort zone. I wondered, was this trip to see Sai Baba really on the path to hidden knowledge? Do I really have to go to such outer limits to discover inner truths? After all, weren't these "inner" truths something I should be able to explore on my own? Why am I here? I asked myself. I didn't mean that question in the philosophical sense, but literally. Why am I here right now?! I felt as though I had made a mistake in coming. Just because a challenge I had made to an Indian mystic had been answered in the most mystical of ways, didn't mean I had to fly to India in hopes of finding my inner self. I could do that on my own, in the comfort of my own country. Maybe it's my training in the martial arts that has made me respond aggressively to a challenge, the challenge of seeking wisdom from an unknown source; I thought as I lay in bed. Martial arts calls for quick reflexes. Had I confused quick physical responses with mental ones?

In the dead of night, being chewed on by bed bugs and mosquitos, I began to ponder my motivation for coming so far. Did I come to explore the unknown? To look at my inner self? To prove that a guru was wrong – or right? Was I looking for God? Was I looking for the meaning of life? Who in the world am I? And why does it have to be answered through the intervention of someone else? Was this just a journey of the ego, one that would confirm my beliefs about myself, a way to prove that I was right about the explorations of the mind I had carried on thus far?

Years later, I realized why I went to India. It was simple. I had to escape myself to know who I truly was. Without searching for self-knowledge in a place I had never been,

I would remain a slave to the ways I had been taught by my upbringing and culture. Unless I went on a journey – literally – I would not have been able to progress past my western training. The act of leaving home to learn something was both a metaphor and a reality. It was like a rebirth. It took me out of the bubble I lived in, and forced me to find a new one, one that was larger and clearer than the one my life had created up to that point. It forced me to expand my world, so I could pass what I had learned to others. It forced me to see my ego for what it was, a grain of sand on a very big beach, where all of the other grains of sand were searching for their own truth, too.

I later realized that I was trying to get lost in another culture, and that it was the best way to find myself and to learn who I truly was, and am.

I wish I'd had the wisdom in those few words on this, my first night in India, but I didn't. I lay there listening to the frightened rhythms of my body, my rapid heartbeat, and my heavy breathing, and I was deeply troubled. I thought about my wife and my children and the thriving practice I was risking by putting it on hold while I chased what? A mystic I had never met? In a culture I had never even read about? Looking back, I realize I had done exactly the right thing. But at the time, I kept asking myself the same question: Why am I here?

And so it went until morning when I shook the bedbugs from my legs, took a cold bucket shower to make certain they were washed off, and did the best I could do with that hole in the floor. Then I waded back into the street and caught a cab the size of a breadbox to get me back to the airport for the next leg of my flight.

This time I boarded a domestic jet to Bangalore in the country's south. The plane was packed with locals, and the notion of checked luggage, or an overhead compartment, seemed lost on the passengers who covered themselves with baggage. India was easier for me to deal with in the daylight, and I soon did what bedbugs had prevented me from doing the night before, I slept.

When I arrived at Bangalore Airport, I collected my bags and made my way out to get a taxi to the hotel I planned to stay in, before I made the final 100 mile journey to Puttaparthi. Puttaparthi is the town that was the site of one of Sai Baba's ashrams. Before leaving the airport terminal I saw my first photo of Sai Baba, a colorful print of the smiling face of the "god-man" set off by his orange robe and a large ball of curly hair. It was taped to the wall of a taxi stall in the airport. I was approached by a taxi driver from the stall who said, "Are you looking to go to Sai Baba's ashram?" I replied, "I am going to Puttaparthi tomorrow, but I am looking for a taxi to my hotel now." With a surprised look on his face, he said, "That hotel is in the opposite direction, why not go straight to Sai Baba, he's in his Whitefield ashram right now, only half an hour away." With that, I took it as a cue and said, "Let's go."

As we left the airport and drove south, I began to see more and more photos of Sai Baba, an indication of just how much this guru was respected by the locals. There are many gurus in India, many of which run chains of ashrams across the country in the way McDonald's runs restaurants. But Sai Baba was unique among his fellow god-men. For one, he was a philanthropist. He had built large hospitals for the poor, headed up major water projects, and built universities. Unlike the self-serving among his practice, Sai Baba seemed to give most of it back in free services to the poor, nurturing them in health and education in a way that the Indian government could not, or would not, do. He also accepted all religions, advising adherents not to drop their previous religious beliefs but instead become better at them. Therefore, he encouraged Catholics to become better Catholics, and Jews to become better Jews. He only wanted to serve as inspiration for spiritual enlightenment, not necessarily the source of it, he said. As a result of accepting one and all, regardless of race, creed, or religious affiliation, he acquired millions of followers worldwide.

That became obvious on the road to his ashram. Pictures of the bushy-headed guru adorned walls and doors along the way to the ashram. And the closer we got to his ashram, the more photos, posters, and even billboards there were. Soon crowds jammed the road, slowing us to a walking pace. Then the beggars and porters crowded against the window, a few at first then dozens, all slapping the window and begging to take my luggage to the nearest hotel.

"Give them nothing," said the driver, speaking in pinched English. "They don't know where you go. Give them bag, and it will disappear."

I left my bags with the driver and walked into the first building I saw; I think it was the visitor's center. "How do I find out about accommodations?" I asked the smiling young man at the reception desk. He merely pointed to the accommodations desk on the other side of the office. I walked slowly across the room, slowing down even more, when I noticed that the two ancient men at the accommodations desk – each easily in their late 80s – were staring at me with shock and disgust.

"Chapel!" shouted one of the men. "CHAPEL!!! CHAPEL!!!"

I froze in my tracks. Chapel?! I had no idea what he was talking about, and didn't have a clue as to why he was angry and shouting "chapel" at the same time.

"CHAPEL!!!" shouted the old man. "CHAPEL!!!"

He pointed at me now and was clearly angry. The other old man at the desk, clearly emboldened by the actions of his partner, set his pencil down, and began yelling the same thing. The veins were literally popping out the sides of his neck.

"CHAPEL!!!, CHAPEL!!!" they both shouted.

Other people at the desk, both Indian and foreigners like myself, began staring at me as I slowly approached the desk. The shouting continued and seemed in no way affected by my shrugs and painful smile. Am I standing in a sacred area of the accommodations office? Am I in a chapel and don't know it? It was like all my years of psychoanalysis had arrived all at once. I went into shock, my only reference to chapel was a church. Had I walked into a church or the wrong building? Somebody pointed at my feet and I realized I was wearing my shoes. Everybody else was in bare feet (in India it is a sign of disrespect to wear shoes indoors).

I go outside and remove them. I lined my shoes up with the others that were outside the door and came back in.

The old man's voice was suddenly so melodious and sweet that I doubted it was the same person.

He waved me past the others and brought me to the front of the line. When I reached into the loose pocket of my combat trousers to collect my passport, he declared "Welcome back Derek". More shock, how did he know my name?

"You have been here many times Mr. Derek and many lifetimes before. Sai Baba has been awaiting your return."

What?! How the man knew my name was a mystery to me. My passport was still in my pocket, and no one in the room knew me except, apparently, the man behind the check-in counter.

I looked at the man at the desk, and then around me at the filthy, overused reception room. I had spent a sleepless night, wondering why I was here. Now I was facing a complete stranger, who yelled at me one moment and welcomed me back to a place I thought I had never been to, the next. I was stunned yet deeply touched at the same time. And I was exhausted. Profoundly exhausted. My spiritual search had left me in a fog of near physical collapse. All I wanted was a hot shower and some sleep, both of which would help me process the long day's events. I took the piece of paper from the accommodations man with the number of my room written on it, and followed his directions to an upstairs room in a nearby building. When I opened the door, I stepped into a 20 x 20 foot room that was fitted with cots for five people. There were another ten on the floor. There was a toilet down the hall and an open bay shower for four people. And "No," one of the room's occupants told me, "There is no hot water in the afternoon, only for a couple of hours in the evening." I put my luggage down and sat next to it. I had slipped deeper into a haze of exhaustion, but the heightened adrenalin from being yelled at had made me too anxious to sleep. I laid down on the floor, but after a few moments, I decided to return to the street and take my first real look at the ashram.

I was on autopilot now, drifting down the street looking at one building after another and admiring the colorful trinkets and clothing for sale in the windows and stalls of the ashram town. There was a certain sameness to all of the stores in that they carried the same products, ones most likely made by the same manufacturer. The main difference between the stores was the enthusiasm of the owners. Some sat behind their cash registers, reading the daily newspaper, and barely looking up when I came in their shop to look at something that caught my eye. Others came right out on the sidewalk and tried to coax me into their shops, telling me they had some item or artifact that none of the other stores had. I made my way down the main street and then came back into the ashram gate. I saw the entrance to a building, there was a part that had no roof, just an open sky, and a big statue of the Goddess Lakshmi. I walked to a part with a tin roof, taking off my shoes, I walked in and saw large life-size photographs of Sai Baba on a wall.

An excellent photographer had clearly taken these pictures. As I was standing there looking at the pictures in a type of trance, I heard a commotion to my left. People were starting to gather. Then two big gates were opened,

I had walked closer to the gates and to my amazement out walked Sathya Sai Baba surrounded by men wearing white. I was so close to him, I put my hand out, "Good to meet you", I said. Sai Baba had a bemused look on his face. Instantly, a hand came across my chest pushing me off balance, nearly falling on my ass. It was one of Sai Baba's sevadals (helpers). When I regained my balance and composure, people were running from every direction towards him. A car was now pulling up for him to get into. As I looked clearly at his face, he smiled or grinned at me, a strange way to say welcome.

For many pilgrims, being attacked by security for being friendly would have been the final insult. Like me, most of the pilgrims had traveled halfway across the world and endured the insults of traveling in a completely foreign environment, to see a guru who somehow had lured them to his ashram. To be knocked on my rear for the act of shaking his hand seemed unwelcoming, to say the least.

Under most conditions, I would have considered such behavior to be a deal-breaker too. But in my brief, no contact meeting with the guru, I experienced a flash of the charisma that made him a great leader. In that moment of eye contact, I sensed a man who saw the past and the future and molded them together to create the present. In his books, he wrote about having no fear of death, and in seeing him I could see in his clear and playful eyes that it was true. It was as though by holding that knowledge of life ever after, he was primed to achieve the incredible, building a world of philanthropy for the omnipresent poor of India. It was in that moment of eye contact – before getting whacked by security – that I saw the meaning of Sai Baba, the man. I was touched immediately.

The day was bright, hot, and dusty. I took a deep breath of India and divided the rest of my day into three tasks: food, shower, and sleep. Tomorrow would be my first Darshan, and I wanted to be fresh for the experience. In its most simple usage, Darshan means sight, as in a beholding. In the world of Hindu worship, it means to have a vision of the divine, or a meeting with a very holy person. The ultimate Darshan is a meeting with God. One such meeting is presented in the *Bhagavad Gita*, an ancient Hindu wisdom poem, in which the warrior Arjuna describes a life-changing visionary encounter with a God.

Hari, the great lord of the possessors of mystic power, then showed to the son of Prithâ his supreme divine form, having many mouths and eyes, having (within it) many wonderful sights, having many celestial ornaments, having many celestial weapons held erect, wearing celestial flowers and vestments, having an anointment of celestial perfumes, full of every wonder, the infinite deity with faces in all directions. If in the heavens, the lustre of a thousand suns burst forth all at once, that would be like the lustre of that mighty one. There the son of Pându then observed in the body of the God of Gods the whole universe (all) in one, and divided into numerous (divisions). Then Dhanañgaya filled with amazement, and with hair standing on end, bowed his head before the God, and spoke with joined hands. [Arjuna said:] O God! I see within your body the Gods, as also all the groups of various beings; and the lord Brahma seated on (his) lotus seat, and all the sages and celestial snakes. I see you, who are of countless forms, possessed of many arms, stomachs, mouths, and eyes on all sides. And, O lord of the universe! O you of all forms! I do not see your end or middle or beginning. I see you bearing a coronet and a mace and a discus—a mass of glory, brilliant on all sides, difficult to look at, having on all sides the effulgence of a blazing fire or sun, and indefinable. You are indestructible, the supreme one to be known. You are the highest support of this universe. You are the inexhaustible protector of everlasting piety.

I doubted my Darshan with Sai Baba would be so complex as this one. This one seemed to have happened spontaneously, an event that had not happened on cue. And it most likely happened when Arjuna was physically alone with his thoughts and spiritual self. The Darshan I would be involved in began at 4 am and was far from being a lonely event. Thousands of people would come, all sitting in orderly lines waiting hours for Sai Baba's arrival.

One of the pilgrims in the crowded room where I was staying had been through many Darshans, and he told me what he knew. He said that the rows where people had to wait became so jammed with people that no one else could join them. At that point, ashram workers had a bag full of discs with numbers on them. They would then hold the bag for the first person in each line to pick a disc, depending on the number on the disc would depend on whether your line was the first to go in, second, and so on. A low number promised a place close to the aisle and a closer view of the guru. To be near the path where he walked, would allow the pilgrim to pass a letter to the guru or even ask him questions, which he may or may not answer.

The man who was telling me about Darshan had been here a dozen times yet had never been close to Sai Baba, not even once. Still, he kept coming, he said, because of the miracles he had seen. I thought the man might have been unbalanced. Traveling halfway around the world a dozen times to only be a distant spectator seemed, at the most insane, and at the least unfulfilling. Still, those in the room around us said they too had come "nine...11....15 times, sometimes twice in the same year..." only to find themselves deep in the crowd where they witnessed only a distant glimpse of the guru.

"One of these days, I expect to have the opportunity to have my own miracle," he said. "But until then, I'm completely taken with everyone else's. Miracles are miracles and worth witnessing, no matter who they happen to." That comment elicited a murmur of agreement in the room and several "Amens." It was clear to me that this man was not the only person here who had been through several Darshans and not been close to the guru. And it was clear that they were all satisfied with the results.

Still not totally understanding the appeal of Darshan, I surrendered to my jet lag and dozed off.

At 3:30 in the morning, people started stirring as the noisy ones in the room began to chant "Darshan...Darshan...." Several veterans got up and made quick beelines for the bathroom. Being first to the bathroom meant they would be first to get in line for the Darshan. I was still in a fog of jet lag when I awoke and for one horrifying moment didn't know where I was, only that there were at least 15 strangers around me struggling to get out of their cots and mumbling "Darshan...Darshan..."

I dressed quickly and walked toward the Darshan hall. I didn't yet know the size of the ashram itself, so I was astounded at the number of people streaming into the facility. I would estimate there were as many as 15,000 people that eventually packed the facility that day. I was told later that this was a small gathering, that a stadium had been built in the ashram to accommodate gatherings ten times that size in Puttaparthi.

I was given a disk with the number "14" on it and was moved to the back of the row. I was approximately 45 feet from the aisle where the guru would pass. From that vantage point, the heads of the people in front of me heavily obscured the aisle he would walk down. When they stood up and began vying for a view, I figured I would see almost nothing of the 5'1" guru.

There I sat for nearly two hours, filled with expectation. Most of these people had never seen Sai Baba up close. On the other hand, I had been lucky enough to see him face-to-face and almost touch him. I still felt somehow that he would single me out, bringing me down to the aisle to walk with him, or at least that he would stop and acknowledge me on his way past as he walked down the aisle. He beckoned me to come to India, I thought to myself, and because of that, I expected some kind of acknowledgment. But even if that didn't happen, I expected a sensation of the miraculous when the guru came into the facility, perhaps even the sense of bells and whistles going off in my head. But that isn't what I got at all. What I got was a very poor view of a small man in orange walking down the aisle, stopping only briefly to take someone's letter or to listen to someone's plea for intercession on one issue or another. He looks like an ordinary guy, I thought as he passed. Why isn't he coming to me? I came around the world to see him! Doesn't he remember looking at me in that room where his security men knocked me on my ass?

To say that I was filled with expectations for this moment, is an understatement (ego). He had known me without seeing me, and now he did not seem to know me after seeing me. My expectations withered as he walked casually down the aisle and turned to walk down another. At that point, I lost sight of him completely. All I could see was the backs of heads bobbing and turning, all trying to see the guru. That's it? I asked myself. That's all I get? Suddenly I was even more thankful for our brief and violent encounter in the gallery the day before. At least it had afforded a moment of direct contact. This Darshan did not meet my expectations. I was disappointed.

When the Darshan ended, I went to the dining hall for breakfast. I was tired, deflated, and dejected. I took a tray of food and sat quietly at a table, watching and listening to the other devotees. Soon I fell into conversation with those at my table and found that they were medical doctors, professors, scientists, and other highly educated professionals. What can these people possibly get out of this guru? I thought. I realized I was becoming disenchanted, and like most who become disenchanted, I didn't try to change my attitude. Rather, it got worse, and soon I began to think about leaving.

After breakfast, I decided to go to the roof of the men's dormitory and figure out whether to leave or stay. The roof was as quiet as a place surrounded by thousands of people can be, but at least I was above it all, able to carry on a good pout while looking down on the massive ashram and the people flowing through its streets. My gaze was interrupted by the shadow of a man that fell over me from behind.

"I am supposed to make you a Reiki master," he said with a heavy Russian accent.

"Supposed to?" I asked.

"Yes, I am supposed to make you a Reiki master."

The Russian was a very pleasant man, tall and confident, with a wise smile on his face and a shock of white hair. He smiled as though he knew me, and was very easy to converse with. He is just the type of person who would be a good Reiki practitioner, I thought. I stood and faced him.

"But I've already studied Reiki," I said.

"Yes," he said. "But I am supposed to teach you advanced Reiki, Karuna Reiki, known as 'open heart'.

If you don't already know, Reiki is a form of energy medicine that was founded in the early 20th century by a Japanese monk. It involves the channeling of universal energy from a master to the patient, and has been assumed to treat a variety of illnesses. The universal energy is most often transferred to the patient through the meditative powers of the master. In fact, most Reiki involves the passing of the hands over the afflicted area instead of touching it, like massage. I had been trained in Usui Reiki, an early form of the practice, but I knew there were more advanced forms of the healing art, including Karuna Reiki, which had improved through the evolution of study as many medical arts do. Although I already used Reiki successfully in my practice, I was interested in learning more advanced forms. As he continued to talk to me about it, I realized that here in India was as good a place as any to study advanced Reiki.

The Russian man and I agreed to meet on the roof the next day after the morning Darshan.

The next morning was another disappointing Darshan. I was closer to the guru this time, but when he passed by, I felt no real connection.

After breakfast, I returned to the dormitory roof to find the Russian gentleman waiting for me. He was a medical doctor in Moscow, he said, an internist who had a special interest in alternative medicine. Over the years, he had studied many different disciplines, including massage, Rolfing, Qi Gong, and a number of other bodywork disciplines. Reiki was studied in Japan and he had returned several times to study all aspects or "lines" of the Oriental art. The line of Reiki he practiced, Karuna Reiki, meant "enlightened spiritual energy meeting," and involved many mysteries that are taught only to the highest masters. My line of practice, Usui Reiki, involved techniques and methods that were open for all to learn. It was his "duty" to teach me some of the mystery techniques of this art.

To do this, he had me sit on two bricks that he had placed on the roof and take some deep yogic breaths. "Accept whatever happens," he told me. Then for the next several hours, he taught me mystery treatments of Reiki, not only by describing them but practicing them on me as well. The lessons he taught me were not only internally intense but apparently, they were externally intense as well. A passing pilgrim told me later that when she looked up on the roof where the private class was taking place, she could see a small cloud over our heads that seemed to be emitting a rainbow.

We had been on the roof for several hours, yet when the teaching ended, I was roiling with energy as though I had been recharged. I found no need to take notes. Rather, I was filled with the Russian man's knowledge, none of which has ever left me. When I asked if I owed him money for the training, he shook me off with a chuckle. "It is my duty," he said. "It was good to meet you and finally fulfill my duty."

There's that word "duty," again, I thought as he walked away. Why did he keep referring to our class work as his "duty"? Hadn't he asked to teach me? Didn't duty imply that he had been asked by someone to teach me the secret arts of Reiki? I wondered what he meant, but I didn't ask. Maybe it's just because he's Russian and he's using the wrong word, I thought. I let it go.

Did I say I have never forgotten any of what he taught me? That isn't quite true. I did forget one thing right away. There were symbols used to perform the Karuna Reiki treatment that required the extra meditative powers that this symbol would provide. I remembered in the middle of the night that I had forgotten to get the symbol and promised myself to get it from the Russian man the next day after Darshan.

The next day's Darshan was another disappointment. I had picked a number that made it impossible for me to even get a glimpse of the guru. I was disappointed when

I left the ceremony and went to breakfast. I picked at my food, dawdled over my coffee, and then went to the Russian man's apartment. I knocked on the door. After a few moments, a Buddhist in robes answered. I told him that I was looking for the Russian doctor and that he had initiated me into a deeper form of Reiki the day before. The man stared at me like I was a ghost. I told him that I needed the special symbol that would allow me to use this particular treatment but had forgotten to get it from him after his teachings. Could he please tell the doctor that I was here?

The Buddhist was transfixed. I soon realized that he had something to say to me; it just wasn't coming out quickly. I stood silently and waited for him to respond.

"I'm sorry to say he has left. His train left an hour ago, and he's flying back to Russia tonight," he said. "But did he tell you why he wanted to teach you advanced Reiki? Because seven years ago, he had an interview with Sai Baba himself who told him that someday a young man will arrive. The guru said, you will know right away that it's the right young man. When you meet him, you should initiate the young man into a deeper knowledge of Reiki. You are apparently that young man."

I was overwhelmed by this revelation.

Lesson: Sometimes Life Is Out of Your Hands

The unexpected happens, and sometimes it takes you exactly where you need to go. It might be uncomfortable getting there, or deep uncertainty might fill your psyche, but once you arrive at this unexpected destination, it may feel like home and the mysterious guidance that took you there may feel like a helping hand from the universe.

I deal with many "control freaks" in my practice, people who think they are in control of their lives and destiny when they are really not so much, at all. When incidents happen that reveal their lack of control – illness, another pig-headed person, or even an airline departure that is late (can you imagine) – they flip out at their lack of control.

Rather than become impotent at their lack of control, I tell my patients to recognize that life meanders like a beautiful river, taking its own direction as it winds to the sea. For some, that's a little too ethereal. If it is, and they look at me with puzzlement in their eyes, I bring it down to this: Your life has a mind of its own, and it's not on your shoulders.

Questions & Answers

Question: Why is it that we have to search for spirituality? Why doesn't it come to us?

Answer: We search because we have forgotten that we are spiritual beings, that everything about us is a spiritual act. We have forgotten that spirit and energy are one and the same. Without energy you cannot live, and without spirit, you cannot survive. They are one in the same thing.

Question: And even more important, how does one search for spirituality without having their life come apart? It seems as though the road to "self" is littered with hurt people.

Answer: One searches for spirituality on a path that is

attractive. It can be a religious path, or one of service to yourself, or to others. It can also be a path of nature, a path of karma, a path of energy healing, and so on. There are many paths in the search for spirituality. And yes, these paths are littered with hurt people, because truth and the search for it, can be painful. That hurt is usually coming from ignorance, or regrets from the past. But pain is often a part of the search that one needs to get over to proceed with their life.

Question: And, exactly what does the search for self mean, and how do we know if we have found ourselves?

Answer: The search for self is the meaning of life: Why are we here? What is the plan? Is there more to life than drinking, eating and sleeping? If so, what? The search for self is a fact-finding mission to answer those questions as best we can.

Question: What should I keep in mind in my own search for self, so I don't hurt my loved ones?

Answer: Well, hurt is something that is perceived and believed. If it is not perceived, or believed, then it's not hurt anymore. Keep in mind that everyone searches for self during their lives. And sometimes in our search, we find that we no longer share common interests with those in our old life. By telling them what you have found you can maybe help them make positive change in their life. Or maybe not. Sometimes the search for self can cause pain for others, and it may not be avoidable.

Question: You took a huge step by following your intuition and going to India. How does one know when intuition should be followed or ignored?

Answer: Like a hot bath, you can test intuition slowly and carefully. Sometimes it turns out to be something you want to avoid, and other times it is an adventure that changes your life.

Question: Your early meetings with Sai Baba didn't meet your expectations, but somehow you pursued this man. What did you see in him at that point? And do we have a right to have expectations of others?

Answer: Well, what I saw at that point, was a man who had done a huge amount of work and had amazing powers on top of it. I saw a very well-organized machine, that was helpful to millions of people around the planet. What I heard, were very practical and easy to understand lessons, that applied to all religions and spiritual beliefs. Like everyone else, I am wired to have expectations of people, but I came to realize that living without expectations was best, because I could see him through a clear lens, one that wasn't clouded by my own expectations. When I removed my expectations, is when I truly began to learn.

CHAPTER 6

Alone in the Crowd

"Love your wife and children and do your
duty towards them as a husband and a father.
But always hold on to the true values. Do not
lose your sense of proportion." Sai Baba

Was I angry? Was I afraid? Was I so desperate for attention that I had created mystical connections in my mind where there were none?

Or was I the chosen child, the lucky recipient of psychic blessings from a guru that would take me on a new path of personal discovery?

Should I ignore these experiences or validate them?

I kept an open mind as I thought about these questions, and because of that, I both victimized and enlightened myself all the way across India and in the airplane back to Ireland. For many hours in the airplane seat, I could not decide whether I was schizophrenic or blessed, a sucker or a winner. Had I been the recipient of divine guidance, or had I just created these experiences in my mind?

About halfway home, I had a flash of understanding that has stayed with me. Rather than being judgmental about the experiences, I should instead feel free to talk about them with my patients. If the experiences were truly genuine, my patients would not only validate them; they would open up and tell me experiences that were fearful to them. And, that's what I did. I immediately integrated my own experiences into my therapy sessions. So, when patients spoke about roads not taken in their lives or intuition or dreams that felt like divine guidance, I would set my notepad down and tell them about the experiences that took me to India. Within days, I realized that a spiritual element had been missing from my practice. By talking about the spiritual events in my life, I was freeing my patients to talk about similar ones in their own.

That was when my practice took off.

Looking back, I call this change "dogma in action" because it freed patients to actually explore the dogma they had been raised with, and to develop their own. I live in Dublin, where the vast majority of my patients are Roman Catholic, a church that thrives on spiritual experience and divine guidance. Yet many Catholics down through history have been shunned for believing they have connected with the divine. In fact, denying the spiritual experiences of parishioners, while asking them to seek them out through prayer and divine intervention, is one of the great contradictions of most western religions. So, despite the fact that much of Catholic dogma came to us through spiritual manifestations, it is extremely difficult to discuss them among Catholic clergy without painful legalistic conversations.

By now, I was inviting patients to freely explore their own spiritual experiences. Rather than consider whether their spiritual experiences were consistent with Catholic dogma, I suggested they stop thinking about religion and first explore how the spiritual events related to themselves alone. Did these spiritual events provide information that will make you live with greater happiness and honesty? Are they going to take you in a healthy direction? If so, I told the patients to write the events down and develop their own dogma by which they could make their lives better. "Dogma is just a set of beliefs you hold true, and they don't have to be related to a religion," I told the patients. "Develop your own dogma and put it into action."

This was a freedom most of my patients had never been given, and they took to the idea with great zeal. Soon I was being told stories and dreams that my patients had told few others.

One of the patients had even had his own experience with Sai Baba! He worked in the Merchant Marines, manning ships that delivered food to India. While in India during one of his voyages, he became critically ill from a bacterial infection and became so sick that he could not return to his ship. Instead, he checked into a street hotel in Mumbai where he curled into a ball on a well-used bed and waited for his illness to subside.

Late that night, a man came into the room and gave him a palmful of ash and told him to eat some and it would make him better. The patient took it and by morning, he was well.

"It was the man in that picture who gave it to me," he said, pointing to a photograph of Sai Baba on my bookshelf.

The patient stopped by the next day with a small pack of vibhuti, the same healing ash given to me by the mysterious disciple at the health expo earlier that year in Kildare. He had kept his vibhuti in a small tin box as a memento of the magic he had encountered in the world.

It wasn't only the patients who liked what India had done to my practice. I liked it too. The combination of Western and Eastern philosophy in psychology made a tremendous amount of sense. I was now enthralled with what India had given me, and I wanted more.

My wife Linda noticed a shift in the way I was relating to her and our children. She didn't like what she saw, and was outspoken about it. She could see that I was pulling away from the family, acting distant, and she didn't like it.

I knew what she was talking about, but there seemed to be nothing I could do. Something had indeed shifted inside of me. I was no longer interested in much of anything, including family. I just wanted to be free of everything – practice, family, house payments – to do whatever I wanted and to advance my exploration of the mystic. To be perfectly honest, I was more interested in moving into a cave where I could explore my mind and the things I had witnessed in India, than in spending time with Linda and the children.

For example, I found myself thinking constantly about the magic that had taken place through Sai Baba, trying to answer its meaning and figure out whether it was truly mystical or just trickery. One of the things that perplexed me the most was the mystery of the "giving discs," discs that constantly emitted a honey-like substance that could be eaten.

Legend has it that a thief encountered Sai Baba and tried to rob him. But rather than be frightened, Sai convinced the thief to build an orphanage on some of his land and take care of children.

"Don't worry about money," he said, giving the now puzzled thief a pair of discs on a string. "When you have need for food, put these discs together and honey, called Amrita, will manifest itself."

The thief did what was suggested of him, putting the discs in a metal container overnight. When he looked inside the container in the morning, it was filled with a honey-like substance that fed the thief, and later the orphans who moved in with him.

People came from far and wide when they heard about the honey-producing discs. Many believed what they saw, while others thought it was a magic trick, one created by the thief to garner donations from the gullible among them.

To prove their authenticity the thief put the discs on the palm of his hand and held it up so the doubtful, as well as believers, could see as the discs began producing large amounts of honey that soon ran like a stream from his hands.

This was one of the famous stories about Sai Baba that made him larger than life in India. But the story of the discs went well beyond just being a story. I had been allowed to hold these discs in the palm of my hand and stood in awe as a quantity of honey filled my hand and began to pour down to the floor. I had a photo taken of my hand filling with honey and my other hand beneath it, catching the overflow. In another photo, I had put a cup in my hand to catch the overflow, and later I had to replace the cup with a bowl.

Now back in Dublin, I spent a lot of time thinking about the miracle of the discs, as well as others I had seen in India. Sometimes I convinced myself that these manifestations were a trick, some sleight of hand that somehow produced massive amounts of honey, or vibhuti, the ash-like manna I discussed earlier that Sai Baba supposedly produced from his bare hands. Then I would look at the photos of me holding the honey-producing discs, or those I had of Sai handing vibhuti to awestruck pilgrims. When I looked at these photos, I realized I was witnessing more than a metaphor; I was witnessing actual proof that the universe can truly provide ones needs if belief is there.

Even though I freely shared my thoughts about the India experiences with my patients, I sometimes wondered if I should discuss these events at all. I felt that I had a healthy fascination with Sai Baba and others like him. He looked normal, and he most certainly wasn't a madman. Sai Baba was just gifted. But still, at times, I feared that my patients would grasp at the "Miracle Man", rather than realizing that what he was "selling" was the realization that one could have miracles in his or her own life, if they could just open up and accept the possibilities.

As it turned out, I did have problems with my patients, although not in the way I expected I would. One time I had an angry husband call me, asking what this "Indian shit" was all about. More than once, an angry spouse (and not always the male) would storm out of couples therapy when I mentioned that the work of Freud and Jung came from Indian mystics 5,000 years earlier, which to me revealed that many spiritual beliefs are at the very core of mankind.

When people became angry at the mention of individual spirituality (an intuitive kind that comes from within), or resented teachings that revealed paranormal experiences and created personal power, I realized they were reacting to a loss of control. If their spouse found personal power in the core of their spirituality, for example, then wouldn't they lose control of that person? And if that happened, what would they control? Themselves? Nothing? Such thoughts bring fear to many people, especially addicts or the like, who have a strong need to control others because they have so little control over themselves.

Despite the anger that references to India raised in some of my patients, I still felt it was important to discuss with them the powers of the human mind so they could access them and not be afraid. Sometimes patients walked away from such talk – they still do – and other times, they came back asking to learn more about what they had rejected. They still do that too. Over the years, I have realized that people know there is more happening in our universe than we are allowing ourselves to experience; they are just in denial, or have no way of knowing how to access it. Their first reaction to confronting the unknown is anger, but eventually, anger turns to curiosity for many and they return to learn more.

For all who fear the unknown but are curious about it nonetheless, I have this quote from one who probed the unknown constantly, Walt Disney, who said, "Around here, we don't look backward very long. We keep moving forward, opening up new doors and doing new things because we're curious...and curiosity keeps leading us down new paths."

***

Sometimes relationships that are growing healthy can look like they are falling apart. That was how my own marriage appeared. It felt that way, too. During the time I was successfully regaling my patients with my newfound psychological discoveries, my own wife was having none of it.

Linda understood why I had been compelled to travel to India. Who wouldn't? By writing a letter to Sai Baba declaring that I would only believe in him if he delivered vibhuti, I had challenged the fates. And when he delivered the requested substance, and did it in such a mysterious way, she knew as I knew that the Indian mystic could not be ignored, and I would have to pursue him to India.

But that was my trip, I was the explorer in the family.

For Linda, life was living as a traditional Catholic, with all the goals of a traditional Catholic wife. She was perfectly happy, staying at home and raising our two children. Where I saw the universe as boundless, she saw it as a comfortable space. She brooded over the children all the time. Where I was on a constant search for self (and still am), Linda did not need to go to India to find what she was looking for. It was all around her, all the time, in the form of a comfortable home, beautiful children, good friends, a good relationship with her mother, and most of all, a general sense of security. She wanted no more than that, as she insisted again and again. She was happy in her world. I was to find out later, she was more awake and spiritual than me, and in fact, believed more than she revealed. She was an extremely powerful being in disguise.

"We have very different thoughts when it comes to spirituality and the big questions about life," she said to me. "But we can live with that."

I said I agreed, but I didn't really. I was witnessing some powerful experiences, and I wanted more. I began to detach from my home life and dream of India and the nature of these experiences. I was spending all of my free time reading books and watching DVDs about the mysteries of the mind, and as a result, I was ignoring my family. In fact, as I told her in so many words, "I am more interested in enlightenment than family."

Linda was stunned by the comment, but she was clearly not surprised. She had obviously been thinking the same thing, too, and now that our true feelings were out on the table, we began to talk about the rift that had grown between us.

Over the next several nights, after dinner was over and our children were in bed, we sat at the kitchen table talking about what we thought was our fracturing relationship. But was actually the beginning of an even stronger relationship, once we worked through our stuff.

Everything was in the open now. I told Linda that I wanted to go to India more frequently to study the mysteries

I was witnessing there. I realized that such a move presented a serious family problem. I had spent a lot of time with our children, taking them fishing and camping and bringing them with me when I practiced martial arts. But I couldn't really bring them along on this journey, I said to Linda, because it wasn't one for children. Linda agreed, but made it a point to remind me that she and the children had needs too, and didn't want them ignored.

We analyzed every aspect of our marriage that we could and came to a Freudian conclusion that many might find familiar: I had married a woman who would be the mother I had always wanted, and she had married somebody to replace her father who had died when she was 10. We were now growing out of that need to replace our parents, and it was strangling our relationship. Calling one another "mother" and "father" were more than terms of endearment. They were how we truly viewed one another, and it was a view that was no longer comfortable to either one of us.

It seemed as though such a conclusion could easily be the end of a marriage. But in our case, it had an opposite effect. We began working to build our relationship on a new foundation. We became the people we really were, instead of acting like we thought parents should act. I'm not going to pretend that this evolution was an easy one. It was, in many ways, wrenching. What I was looking for was the freedom to explore the world, and this exploration didn't necessarily involve my family. Rather, it involved discoveries about the world that I had made since having a family. I wanted to explore places, mysteries, and concepts, that were now completely occupying my mind, and vying for the attention that my family craved and deserved. I felt guilty about this desire to explore this new world and knew my openness with Linda was painful for her, but I also felt that being honest was the best policy. Without honesty, there would be no opportunity to build a new foundation in place of the one that was crumbling.

"We married very young," she said during one of our evening talks. "There is no reason we shouldn't expect to rebuild our marriage several times in our lives."

Looking back, I see how generous she was. My family was, in fact, the most important thing in my life. I loved our children very much and would do anything for them. I worked very hard at times, doing two or three jobs to get money. Linda and I were madly in love; even through this, the love never changed, just the story had to. We both had to be free to be together fully and empowered. This we did by agreeing to renew our marriage vows, acknowledging that the vows we had taken at ages 19 and 21 no longer applied. We wrote wedding vows that removed the boundaries from our relationship. And I do mean, "we." By now, Linda recognized several changes she wanted to make in our relationship, too. Sometimes I felt as though her changes were a bit of "Irish Alzheimers," where we forget everything but our grudges, but I came to realize that those grudges were honest concerns for her that needed to be dealt with in our vows.

I pushed Linda hard to go to India with me. It was only by going there, I told her, that she could truly understand the mysteries I was dealing with and why I was drawn to them. She finally agreed to fly to India, where a priest would marry us again with new vows.

I looked forward to this marriage of renewal, not only because it represented a healthy change in our lives, but because I wanted her to see the mysterious world of the Indian ashram, and understand the magical ways and spiritual teachings of Sai Baba. I admit I had a deep belief, and disbelief, in Sai Baba at the same time. I had witnessed miracles and disappointment, and had seen horror and beauty, all at the same time at the ashram. The world of this guru seemed to be one of riches surrounded by poverty, wisdom laced with ignorance, attachment linked with detachment. It was a world where the guru's stated goal was to "help one desire less", yet his own life was laden with material goods it seemed.

I saw the spirituality that permeated from Sai Baba's world but also the hypocrisy. And, although, I spoke confidently to my patients about the untapped powers of the human mind that could bring magic and miracles to their lives, I wasn't completely sold in the belief that Sai Baba was the way to understand them. That was really why I insisted that Linda come with me to India. I needed the closest person in my life to help me understand my feelings toward this strange little mystic. I needed my wife's opinion.

As it turned out, her opinion was not good.

For one thing, she couldn't reconcile the gold statues and other trappings of wealth and power that surrounded the guru, with the stark poverty that existed outside the walls of the ashram.

"People are starving to death out there," she said to me after an afternoon walk revealed this horror to her. "If he cares so much, why doesn't he spend his gold on feeding the hungry?"

I had no answer.

At the Darshan, (the morning meetings with Sai), Linda sat on the women's side of the aisle. Since no one told her to pick a number, she found a seat every day in the VIP section of the hall. And every day, Sai would stop at the VIP section and commune with the dignitaries. Linda was sitting right before him, able to hear his every word and feel his presence.

When I found out she'd had such close access to Sai, I asked her what it was like to be in the presence of the master. Had he spoken to her? Did he impart wisdom? Did magical things happen? Did unexplained experiences happen to her later?

She just shook her head when I asked these questions. "I felt nothing special," she said.

Linda felt nothing special because she thought Sai was a con man. She would point at the buildings and say they should be living space for the poor, instead of curio shops catering to spirit-seeking pilgrims. And then there was the gold. Linda couldn't put the gold behind her. Every time she saw a golden statue, or a regal chair covered with gold leaf, Linda shook her head.

"I can't understand all of this wealth amidst all of this suffering," she said. "There are people starving out there right under our noses, and a few chips of this gold could feed them for their lifetime. But it just sits here and collects dust while people starve."

I reminded her of the Catholic Church, and many other religious or spiritual movements, and all of the wealth they held. "There's more wealth in the Catholic Church than in the coffers of most countries," I said.

"I can't argue with that," she said. "But the poverty here is crushing. Crushing! Did you see those children out there! They are all skin and bones."

Lesson: Your belief systems will be tested

I know what she said was true, but what I saw was human nature in action. When Westerners started following Sai, they wanted to show their appreciation for his teachings and miracles, I said to Linda. And in doing that, they donated buildings, vehicles, gold, and other trappings of Western wealth. Sai called it "tinsel and trash," and knew that it was contradictory to the way in which Jesus lived. But he also understood human nature and realized that people are drawn to tinsel and trash. "I bring people in with tinsel and trash," said Sai Baba. "And I teach them spirituality."

"Take a look at the Vatican," I said. "All of those expensive buildings and statues are contrary to the teachings of Jesus. Yet people are spiritually energized by them. It's the way most humans are."

"Not me," she said. "This is making me sick."

The next day Linda was walking through the ashram when about 20 trucks roared by and out the front gate. In the bed of these trucks, a number of young boys held massive pots, with steam pouring out of them.

"What was that?" she asked a German woman who had also stopped to watch the spectacle.

"Oh, those are the feeding trucks," she said. "Every day, Sai Baba has trucks go into the surrounding villages twice a day to feed the poor."

"That's very nice," said Linda.

"It is amazing," said the woman. "People elevate Sai Baba and build this huge, rich ashram, yet he is not really interested in living in luxury. In spite of this, he still has a room that is 10 feet by 10 feet and contains only a chair, writing desk, and piece of cloth on the floor for his bed. Sai Baba is a very puzzling man."

Linda felt better about Sai Baba after that conversation, but she still didn't need to go to India to find what she was looking for. Her best life – the life she was looking for – was right in the middle of Dublin.

Try as I could, I couldn't place my heart in Dublin. My wife and children were there, my siblings and patients, my house, and my friends. I loved them all very much. But I was discovering other worlds, and investigating phenomenon, and I didn't feel as though I could do that in the city of my birth, not with all that had happened in my life, and with what I had become. I didn't know yet, that was something I had to create and could not be found on a map, and I was ready to go look for the Derek O'Neill that I thought existed out there. I was ready to go search for enlightenment.

Looking back on these events, I think my childhood had caught up with me. I had seen my family disintegrate before my very eyes, largely because of the temptations of the world. My father had been tempted by other women, which drove my mother to drink. My mother had become seduced by alcohol and was lost to the family. My brother was abused by priests driven by their own temptations and lost his faith in God and mankind. Temptations could take our lives away from us in a minute. As Sai Baba said, "When you give up totally, the temptations will fade." I found myself giving up totally. I found myself seeking a life with no attachments. I found myself trying to rise above body consciousness and seek insightful vision. I wanted to see myself.

I told Linda my feelings. She was remarkably accepting of how I felt. She understood the burden of my childhood more than I did, and realized that the only way for us to truly be together was to let me go back to India and continue my search.

And what did that search consist of? Was I attempting to fill a void in my life? Was I trying to shake an inner weight that was holding me down? Was I forcing myself to reach for a meaning to life that might not exist? Was I neglecting my family in a selfish pursuit? The answer to all of these questions was "yes." And although I boarded a jet that was headed for Delhi, I didn't know my final destination, just my goal to better understand the mystical world around me so I could give that understanding to others.

***

I arrived at Delhi, caught a plane to Bangalore, a cab to Puttaparthi, and had a fitful night's sleep in a room full of strangers at the ashram, before arising at sunup for the daily Darshan.

I skipped breakfast to get there early and drew a number that put me next to the carpet where Sai Baba would pass. I was lucky – or maybe blessed – to draw such a number. It was only from such a vantage point that I could maybe hope to have him answer the questions I had written on a piece of paper that was folded in my shirt pocket.

As the stadium filled, I began to perspire with nervousness. Shaking with anxiety, I pulled the paper from my pocket and unfolded it to read the simple questions I had asked.

*Should I leave Ireland and move to India so I can better understand the mystery and magic that I have seen here?

*Should I give up martial arts so I can devote more time to the mystical studies?

The second question may seem an odd one, but to me, it was important. I had practiced martial arts since I was young. They were undoubtedly what kept me stable throughout my teenage years, as well as away from drugs. Without the physical and mental discipline of martial arts, I don't think my life would have turned out so well.

Now I had a martial arts club where I trained as many as 200 students per week. I knew I was doing good by teaching the discipline of martial arts to young people, but I also knew it took a tremendous amount of energy for me to teach, and by doing that, I was not devoting enough time to my own studies. Or at least I thought. As a finite being, I needed guidance – lots of guidance – but at this point, I was hoping to get these two important questions answered.

When it seemed as though they couldn't pack more people into the hall, the music started, and Sai Baba walked in. He was far away, and from where I was sitting, he looked very small. Surrounded on both sides by giant security men, he walked slow and relaxed as though he was the only person in the entire hall.

His presence was like electricity in the stadium. Some people wept. Others held their hands to their mouths and just stared, as though they had seen the messiah. People on either side of the carpet handed him notes that were passed on by Sai Baba to others behind him. They would immediately put the letters in a bag and keep them for later. I assume that the guru read at least some of them. There was no way he could read them all since he would have hundreds of notes by the end of each daily Darshan.

I had my note in my hand hoping to hand it to him too, but as he approached, I noticed that a bright green grasshopper had crawled out from the audience and was now sitting on the carpet directly in front of me. I pushed the insect with my finger, hoping he would hop away. But he didn't, instead, he sat there, right in the path of Sai Baba's entourage.

As they approached, I put the note back in my pocket and cupped my hand, putting it over the top of the grasshopper to make sure nobody in Sai Baba's entourage stepped on it.

The first two security guards stepped over my hand, which put Sai Baba directly in front of me. He stopped for a moment when he saw my hand. Then to my surprise, he began gently pushing my hand with his foot. It was a playful push, as though he was poking a kitten with his toe. I looked up at him. He was talking with someone behind me in the third row, but still, he focused on my hand, nudging it with his toe until my hand and the grasshopper were off the carpet. With a flip of his toe, my hand went up, and the grasshopper flew away.

He looked at me and smiled as he walked away. Then, a few feet away, he looked back and smiled again. And then, a few feet farther, he looked back again and nodded and smiled. I didn't know what to make of the silent attention, but I smiled back. A few more feet down the carpet, he looked back to nod and smile again.

When Darshan ended a woman ran across the carpet and grabbed my arm.

"He was giving you a message," she said excitedly.

"What do you mean?" I asked.

"The kicking of your hand and then repeatedly looking back. It wasn't about getting your hand off the carpet or saving the grasshopper; it was a message!"

Others gathered around. They had interpreted the guru's actions as a message too and wanted to know what I thought it was.

"Did you give him a letter or a note?" one of them asked. "What did you ask for?"

I remembered my note and felt for it in my pocket. It was still there. I remembered the questions I had asked, too: Should I leave Ireland and move to India? Should I give up martial arts so I can better study mysticism?

I was truly puzzled now. Did his actions answer my questions? What could protecting a grasshopper mean in relation to my questions? And why was he kicking my hand away from the grasshopper?

With my mind consumed by questions, I stepped into the river of people leaving the stadium, a lone pilgrim among many, together, yet all on our own journey.

Questions & Answers

Question: You mentioned suspending judgment about experiences that are mystical. I have had experiences that seem mystical, but I always judge them to death. Still experiences that seem to be mystical keep happening. How do I learn to suspend judgment, so the true nature of an experience can be revealed?

Answer: By suspending judgment, you are widening your consciousness to see the bigger picture. An example of training to achieve this would be calling in an angel. And just at that moment a car drives by, the sun hits the mirror and shoots a light through the window onto the wall. You may at that stage believe you had just seen an angel manifest. It doesn't mean you have, and it doesn't mean you haven't if you suspend judgment. Your belief could bring you to your destination. By allowing all events to just happen, and registering your response to them with discernment, this suspends judgment, as judgment is close-minded and discernment is open.

Question: You seem to be a great believer in dreams as a means of self-revelation. How do I know when my dreams have meaning and when they are just dreams?

Answer: There is no such thing as "just dreams." Dreams are the royal road to information. The function of dreams is to alleviate anxiety that would have been built up during the conscious activity of the day. But as we know from many stories, dreams fill in the gaps to create your whole story, i.e. if you're not confident in your waking state, you may have a lot of dreams showing you are a very confident individual.

Question: I recently went to Egypt and felt transformed by the experience. When I returned, I was more interested in my personal transformation than in my job or family. You mention having this kind of "shift" too. I don't like it. Is there a way to return focus to my family but not lose sight of my transformation, too? I love them both.

Answer: When you have an awakening, the excitement drives you forward without you looking at the consequence of what you're leaving behind. The best way is to take time out of your excitement to see what's going on in your daily life, and then jump back into that fresh river of excitement again. Remember, there is something good in your awakening for your family and friends, too.

Question: There are great miracles in the world. You mention at least two of these in this book, Sai Baba's ability to create vibhuti, and the discs that keep creating a honey-like substance. There are many more, of course, all over the world. Why aren't these experiences discussed in the popular press? If everyone knew about them, wouldn't such knowledge change the world for the better?

Answer: There are many great miracles in the world. To my way of thinking, the greatest miracle may be a single mother working three jobs to send her children to school, and to feed them and keep them out of trouble. That's a miracle, and an all too common one. The vibhuti and the honey on the other hand is so overwhelming that doubt has to arise, because the inability to suspend your belief will cause that doubt. Until such a time as science and spirituality test this phenomena there is no basis for anybody to believe, except those who do.

Question: Is there something in our childhood that causes us to be dissatisfied with our lives? Can a person with a bad childhood ever find true spiritual happiness?

Answer: It is never too late to have a good childhood. With time comes knowledge and wisdom. The knowledge of who we really are, and what we can really achieve, is what we should strive to attain. It will eliminate all the unnecessary suffering of not having this knowledge.

Question: Sai Baba seemed to answer your questions metaphorically, if at all. Why don't wise men answer questions directly?

Answer: Because they feel it is not their mission to do your homework for you, because this would, actually, take power from you. They also have come to realize that our mind is set up to understand metaphors, and if we struggle a little for the answer, we will learn more, and the lessons will stay with us longer.

CHAPTER 7

Signs and Symbols

"Kwai Chang Caine: He is a beggar, like the
rest. I can see he is greatly in need of food. But
he does not eat. Master Po: He seeks to satisfy a
stronger hunger. "
From TV series Kung Fu

I rarely slept well when I was at the ashram. Despite being exhausted from the travel to Puttaparthi, I found my mind constantly engaged by the mysteries I witnessed, or heard about from the other pilgrims. So, although my body was exhausted, my mind stayed active and prevented me from sleeping, until I finally passed out only a few hours before the sun came up, and it was time to rise once again.

So, it was again this night. As a roomful of strangers breathed the deep breath of sleep all around me, I lay in my narrow bed and pondered the question that had been with me all day: What was the message of the freed grasshopper?

My mind probed many topics in search of the answer, until it finally shut down and I fell asleep. By the time

I awoke, I was convinced that the entire incident had meant nothing, and that the guru was merely kicking my hand out of his way to make certain no one stepped on it. As Groucho Marx once said about all of the sexual references in Freudian psychology, "Sometimes a cigar is just a cigar." Perhaps a grasshopper is just a grasshopper, I thought to myself. Or a hand is just a hand. I was befuddled and I just wanted to let go of the topic.

The next day I ate breakfast, went to Darshan where I drew a number far away from the carpeted aisle, and then returned to the room. That was when I started thinking again about the grasshopper incident. I knew it meant something and whatever it meant was at the very top of my mind.

I lay down on the bed and began to drift toward the unconscious. For a split second my life flashed before me, going rapidly backwards to my youth where it stopped – froze for a moment – so I could see the image it delivered. I awoke with a start and shouted out what I had seen.

"David Carradine!!!"

Other people in the room jumped. Some laughed at the thought of hearing the television actor's name. Others stared at the strange man who was now sitting on the edge of his bunk, laughing, and shaking his head.

"David Carradine!!" I said again.

"Kung Fu!" shouted an American who was flat on his back from jet lag.

We both laughed out loud, albeit for different reasons.

Although it was my brother-in-law who had first introduced me to the martial arts, it was the 1970s television series Kung Fu that kept me interested.

In that show, David Carradine played Kwai Chang Caine, an orphaned American of mixed parentage, who found himself in a Chinese monastery after his parents died in China. There he was taught the art and spiritual power of Kung Fu by Master Po, who was blind yet had an uncanny ability to see the world through his other senses. Master Po was endlessly patient with the young Caine, who he addressed as "Grasshopper."

Typical of the exchanges in the weekly series was this one between Master Po and David Carradine, aka "Young Caine."

Master Po: Close your eyes. What do you hear?

Young Caine: I hear the water. I hear the birds.

Po: Do you hear your own heartbeat?

Caine: No.

Po: Do you hear the grasshopper which is at your feet?

Caine: Old man, how is it that you hear these things?

Po: Young man, how is it that you do not?

To anyone in martial arts, the television series was motivational. It is my guess that tens of thousands of young boys, like myself, signed up for Kung Fu classes based on that series. And although few of us stayed in the classes for long, the image of David Carradine in that role will stay with us for our lifetime.

It was indeed with me now. I could imagine young Caine walking through the American west, constantly being challenged by tough cowboys for his Chinese style of clothing, or the ponytail that sprouted from the back of his bald head. Clothing and hair were the source of persecution, and wisdom and strength were the way out of it, for young Caine, or "Grasshopper" as the monk called him.

Now in my adulthood, I was thinking of Grasshopper again, realizing that my intuition was coming up with the same thing. I now knew what Sai Baba was thinking when he kicked my hand off the carpet and flipped it up so the grasshopper beneath it could hop away. "Let it go," he was telling me. "You have practiced martial arts long enough. Let it go and then you can go deeper."

I lay back down on the floor and thought about the hours I had spent practicing for martial arts competitions. I trained to stave off the anger I had at my mother, trained to avoid drugs, and trained to stop thinking. I trained and competed for every reason I could think of. I had even become so good by the age of 23, that I would have made it to the Irish Olympic team had I not broken an arm. That kept me from competing in the 1988 Olympics.

With others, I helped found a martial arts club where we changed the lives of street kids who needed discipline, and an outlet for their anger and energy. Now I was being asked by a guru to leave martial arts, or at least, that's what I thought I was being asked to do.

Could this man possibly know me well enough to ask me to quit martial arts? I asked myself. I had my doubts, but they disappeared the next day at a café in the marketplace.

I had taken a walk around the ashram with three other pilgrims and now, hot and sweaty, we went to this tiny clutch of tables and ordered a large bottle of water. The waiter brought four empty glasses and a plastic bottle of water that was hot from being stored in the midday sun.

"What I wouldn't do for an ice cream cone, or a glass of cold water," I said, pouring the water into the glasses.

Almost immediately the glasses began to mist, sweating from their cold contact with the damp air around us. Mine became so cold that a layer of ice formed on top.

"Jesus," said the American at the table. "WTF?"

I was speechless. Another miracle was taking place in front of me. I knew my days of marital arts were over, for the time being, at least.

And that was when things started to happen.

In Ireland, I was meditating with a group when Sai Baba appeared to me in a vision. He walked behind me and pushed me forward so my chest was pressed against my quads and knees. Then he drew a complex symbol down my spine that charged me with bliss, light, elation, and fire, all at the same time. Then he came to a place in front of me and showed me how to draw the symbol. Then he disappeared.

A few minutes later, the leader of the meditation group brought us back to consciousness.

"Does anyone have anything to share?" she asked.

She looked around the meditation circle and focused on me.

"Derek, do you have anything to share?"

I paused a moment. The visionary encounter was so vivid that I thought the other members of the group would think I'd had a break with reality. "No," I said.

"Derek?" she asked. She didn't believe me.

With that challenge, the truth poured out.

"Sai appeared to me right now, during our meditation," I said. "He drew a symbol on my spine that he said would awaken the heart, if drawn on another person. He said that the reason there are so many heart attacks is because people are bypassing the heart chakra. When that happens, they either become too academic and lose their emotions, or they become very materialistic and become reliant on things like material goods or sex; anything that makes them feel good."

A buzz traveled around the meditation group as different members asked me to draw the symbol on them. I refused. I was still dazed from the visionary encounter with Sai, and didn't want to detract from the effects of that encounter.

There was, of course, the one person in the group who would not take "no" for an answer. Her name was Andrea, a spunky 40 year old, with a lot of energy and a bad limp caused by a car accident 15 years earlier. Her left leg was slightly bent from the bone-breaking trauma and appeared weaker than the other. She stood in front of me and insisted I draw the symbol, and when I said "no", she demanded.

I drew the symbol carefully. The symbol is explained at: derekoneill.com/symbolism-of-the-prema-agni

When I finished drawing the symbol she fell to the floor. Her eyes rolled into the back of her head, and she began to froth at the mouth, and shake violently. I was afraid she was dying.

A nurse who was in the group took control and soon Andrea had her eyes open, and was speaking very loudly about her leg, and the power she had felt after I drew the symbol.

Andrea sat in a chair for a moment and then sprang up. "I have to go! I have to go!" she said, pushing through the group.

We all thought she was headed out the door, but that wasn't the case. Andrea began walking rapidly around the meditation group, which had now fallen silent and was watching her in disbelief.

"It's my leg!" she said excitedly. "I'm not limping anymore!"

After that, the meditation group begged me to draw the symbol on their body. I decided not to draw the symbol on anyone for some time after that. What happened, had actually frightened me, and I decided to keep the symbol to myself for a while.

Then the dreams started. It was early October, and I had them night after night. In them, Sai appeared and said,

"The time is now, the time is now. Come and see me. The time is now."

In one of the dreams, he is standing in a shop in Puttaparthi holding a watch, and saying, "The time is now." Behind his shoulder is a Christmas tree.

I got the idea that Sai wanted me to return to the ashram at Christmas, which was totally out of the question. Christmas was big in our family because it was the only time that our entire family got together. The idea that I would leave for India during this hallowed holiday would never enter my mind on its own. I didn't mention the dreams to Linda, nor their content, since the mention of going to India over the holidays would have caused a war on the home front.

Still, though, the dreams continued. And one morning, as I lay in bed pondering the latest one, Linda rolled over and said, "I just had a dream of Sai Baba. He came to me and told me to tell you that he wants you in India for Christmas."

I didn't even think about the supernatural nature of what had just happened. Instead I became angry.

"I've been having the same dream," I said. "I think Sai is asking too much. There's no way I'm going to India for Christmas."

"You have to go," she said sternly. "I can tell that Sai has an important message for you."

"Isn't going to happen," I said, getting out of bed.

I had breakfast and then went to my office/healing center in my home to begin my workday. I went to my appointment book to scan the list of patients coming that day and tried to ignore the poster of Sai Baba that hung on a wall behind me. Finally, I gave in and turned to the poster.

"You know I have no money," I said to the grinning guru. "So, here's the deal. If all of this is not in our imagination, if you really want me over there, then not only do you have to buy me a ticket, but you have to buy it and put it right into my hand. Then I'll believe it's real."

Since I was alone in the room, I gave Sai a dressing down. I told him that he shouldn't have given me the symbol, and all of the responsibility that came with it. Having such a powerful symbol was too frightening for me, and besides, I was not good enough to have such a powerful symbol.

"Give it to somebody who is good, not somebody who eats meat and drinks Guinness," I said.

I came out of my office/healing center and went into the house where I flicked on the television and sat down. The Song of Bernadette was playing, the story of the young visionary in Lourdes, France who had eighteen visions of the Virgin Mary. She suffered mightily after telling the townsfolk about what she saw. Yet through her suffering she gained redemption. Is this movie another sign? I asked myself, turning the television off and returning to the healing center.

Later that afternoon Linda returned from shopping and handed me an airline ticket.

"I saved up a few Euros for us to go on holiday but I'm giving it to you for Christmas," she said.

At that moment, I realized that our marriage had changed. It was as though we had given each other permission to be who we were, without it being a threat. We were looking at the same path and headed toward the same destiny. We had progressed enough that we didn't need to depend on one another in a cold, dependent, and unhealthy way anymore. We had literally freed ourselves from one another, and in doing so, were closer than ever.

"Thank you," I said, too moved to say more. Two weeks later I was on the plane and on my way to India.

***

I would have thought there would be less people in the ashram due to Christmas. But when I checked into my sleeping quarters, the bunks were almost entirely occupied by Westerners who decided to spend their holidays in India, instead of at home with their families. As for guilt about this decision, there appeared to be none. The pilgrims were happy to be there and showed it with laughter and good cheer.

On Christmas morning we awoke early and went to the ashram mandir. I got into line. There was a definite buzz of energy around the place; after all it was Christmas Day. This was the year 2000, the Millennium, and I expected today to be a day of great change in my life. Even though I had only relied on dreams and visions to come over, I was by now a true believer that he was divine and could communicate with us in this way. While I was sitting there, a fire was lit on the stage and people began to sing Christmas carols. It was very moving and beautiful. When they began to sing "O Holy Night" a shiver went up my spine, I felt like I left my body and began to feel what it must have been like to be an apostle of Jesus.

When the Christmas carols ended people stood up to leave. I was very confused as I was expecting Sai Baba to come out. "Why are people leaving?", I asked a man beside me, and he said, " Oh that's it, Darshan is over". Boy, did I get angry. He had dragged me all the way here from Ireland for Christmas Day and this was it, a fire. I stood up, angry, and was walking out of the mandir fast, when a sevadal grabbed me by the arm and sat me in lines that were forming saying, "Queue here for Darshan". It was then I realized that the fire was just preparation for the physical Darshan of Sai Baba. When the numbered discs were drawn, I found myself in the first line, the one next to the red carpet. The music started and I could see Sai in the distance walking, in the midst of his security people and handlers. I have to write down what I want, I thought. Asking the man next to me for a pen, I pulled a piece of paper from my back pocket and drew the symbol. I began to communicate telepathically with Sai Baba:

"If this symbol really came from you, please take this piece of paper and I will know that it's real. If not, ignore me and I will work on my ego."

The guru got closer and then he was standing right in front of me, addressing someone in the crowd behind me. And then, just like that, he was across the carpet and moving away. I've lost him, I thought. My attention went to the note, which I was now sticking up my sleeve, so no one would notice my obvious neediness to have him read it. When I looked back up, he had doubled back and was heading straight for me. Before I could catch my breath, he was standing before me, a smile across his lips.

"Derek," he said. "Give me the Prema Agni." In shock, I reached up my sleeve and handed him the note.

"This symbol will help build 77 healing centers," he said, bending close. "When the world economy collapses – and it will – build 77 healing centers. You build them and I will fill them to capacity."

Healing centers…build them and he will fill them?…What the hell is a healing center? Why 77 of them? Before I could process the questions and get them out of my mouth, he was 20 feet down the carpet. He looked back, waved and grinned, and then turned to focus on what was ahead of him. Will puzzles never cease? I thought, as the only man who could truly answer these questions about the centers walked farther away.

I stayed another week at the ashram but at no time did I get close to Sai Baba or, for that matter, close to figuring out what he meant by "healing centers." I had only the one cryptic meeting with him that left me energized yet confused.

I returned to Ireland with a huge question mark dangling over my head. What am I supposed to do? I told Linda about the meeting with Sai and the 77 healing centers he told me to build. She was as puzzled as I was and asked the same questions.

"Why 77 centers?" she asked.

"He didn't provide that information," I said. "He only told me the number I was to build."

"So, what is a healing center, anyway?" she asked.

"You've got me," I said. "He didn't provide any information about that, either."

Linda suggested I focus on the purpose of the healing centers, and that's what I did. After all, I knew how many healing centers I was supposed to build; I just didn't know what they were.

The first idea that came to mind was a large meditation center where hundreds of people would come together and meditate on such problems as depression and anxiety. Those were among the most prevalent problems I dealt with in my practice, so I thought those should be the focus of the centers. I then realized that a "large" meditation center equaled big problems, including rent and management. Does he want these to be smaller facilities? I wondered. I focused on creating centers that were home based, perhaps a living room program where individuals opened their home to devotees once or twice a week. It would be there, I reasoned, that like-minded people would come together for fellowship and to ponder pertinent issues of individuals and the world.

Then I made the concept of healing centers even more simple, reducing it down to loyal followers of Sai Baba who might go door-to-door like Jehovah's Witnesses, asking people if there were any "issues" they had that meditation might help.

And so on, and so on. Nothing seemed right to me, and since I wasn't given a clue by Sai Baba, I was left with the frustration of guessing what the guru wanted. In typical fashion, I was left to ponder a tiny piece of the puzzle without knowing what the entire puzzle was supposed to look like when it was assembled.

Then all of that changed. A few months after my Christmas meeting with Sai, a woman showed up at my Dublin office talking about a message she had received in a dream. The host of the dream was Sai Baba, she said. He stood before her in his orange outfit and with a lilt of happiness in his voice, told her about my mission and my dilemma, namely that I didn't know what a healing center was.

"The purpose of healing centers is to reach the movers and the shakers of the world and get them to begin to understand what is really going on in the world economy, so we can begin to adjust it before 2023," he said. "Now tell Derek what he is supposed to do, so he can get on with it." This sparked a remembrance of Swami saying the date 2019-2020 would be the beginning of the economy collapsing.

In essence, I was a "seed", a person whose goal would be to assemble people with the ability to meditate and brainstorm on ways to fix the world.

I began to study the words and teachings of Sai, and talk to other followers about the nebulous task that had been given to me. Through these studies, I discovered the meaning of "77" for the number of healing centers I was to establish. Sai's belief was that we have 77 energy points in our body, all of which are linked to our chakras, or pranas, the centers of our life force. He was calling for 77 healing centers, because he wanted one for each energy point. Or so I thought.

Although founding 77 of anything seems like a lot of work, Sai believed it would take no time at all for these centers to form once it became clear that we were headed for the calamity around 2020 to 2023. It will be that year, said Sai, that a crisis point will be reached, one that will force us to decide who on the planet will be allowed to live and die.

Population and resources will be the issue, as global warming, lack of water resources, and a rapidly growing world population, will leave first world nations to decide which third world, and lifeboat nations will be forced to survive on rationed resources, and possibly even die. At that point, the world will be at a physical and spiritual crossroad, where the people will have to decide which way they want to live, by sharing and caring, or having to decide who will live and die.

Such a crisis isn't necessary, said Sai, as long as we can learn to live with less. That would be my job, and the thousands of other "seeds" who had been targeted by Sai Baba to start thousands of meditation centers aimed at the enlightenment of mankind, in the hope that it will consume less so that others might survive.

And how was I to teach people how to consume less? What was my textbook? I had read most of the discourses of Sai, but I realized that reading and understanding his wisdom was easy. What was not easy was teaching it to others. Sai was, of course, the best at teaching his beliefs because they came organically from him. But before I could start even one center, I had to be able to convey Sai's teachings with a spiritual power that would make it stick in the mind of the beholder. To do that, I needed to watch him in action. I had to return to India.

Doing this would not be easy. I now had many more patients than I had before my last trip to India. My exposure to Sai's teachings, and my visits to his ashram, had changed me as a psychotherapist. Thanks to my exposure to Sai, the dogma of my limited schooling had melted away. I became a better listener and found myself learning as much from my patients as they did from me. These patients recommended me to others, and soon my practice was highly successful.

Between a thriving practice and a busy home life, I was afraid that I would not be able to find the time to return to India. When I explained my concerns to Linda, she just shook her head.

"Derek, you bought the ticket when you first went to India. Now you have to stay on the train until it gets where it's going," she said. "Getting off in the middle of a ride is not a good idea."

With that truth lodged in my mind I made arrangements to return to India again.

***

I returned to India three or four times a year for the next several years. In that course of time I studied many things. I read the works of Sai Baba, studied the way he structured his organization, watched how he conducted himself in public, and admired the beatific simplicity with which he conveyed his wisdom.

There were many things I never understood about Sai Baba. The vibhuti that appeared out of his fingers like ash was always a mystery to me. The endless supply of honey that came from the discs was remarkable. But among the most amazing of things to me was the way he conveyed information to someone who needed it. It was as though he would give someone a message and they would carry it to you at a time when you had somehow peaked, or had become confused and desperately needed information. That was when the person would show up and deliver the information so that once again you could be on your way. Information came mysteriously, and on a need-to-know basis, yet almost always on time.

That happened to me with some of the most important information I ever received from Sai Baba, the five human values. These are what the centers should be based on.

The Five Values

The five values were not created by Sai. Rather, they are the principles that form the backbone of the great religions of Christianity, Islam, Judaism, Buddhism and Hinduism. Here are the five values as outlined and described by Sai Baba in his discourses. The titles include the Sanskrit word for each value:

Truth (Sathya)

"Truth is that which is not modified by time, space or attribute. It is the same forever, unaffected and unchanging; it is never proved false by some subsequent event or knowledge."

"Have faith that truth will save you in the long run. Stick to it regardless of what might befall."

"Don't have hypocrisy or crookedness in your speech. Both unpleasant truth, and pleasant untruth, have to be avoided. Sathya (Truth) is God Himself."

Right Conduct (Dharma)

"Every profession, every stage of life, each gender, each period of life as fixed by age – childhood, boyhood, adolescence, youth, middle age, old age – has duties and obligations, which set the norm and guide the individual to benefit himself and society."

"Practicing what you preach, doing as you say it has to be done, and keeping practice in line with precept. Earn virtuously; yearn piously; live in the reverence of God, live for attaining God; that is Dharma."

"See no evil - see what is good.
Hear no evil - hear what is good.
Speak no evil - speak what is good.
Think no evil - think what is good.
Do no evil - do what is good.
This is the way to God."

Peace (Shanti)

"Peace is the stage in which the senses are mastered and held in balance. To experience peace, we must overcome our excessive desires and unreasonable expectations. Agitation usually results from unfulfilled desires, not from external conditions."

"When man thinks, speaks, and acts along virtuous lines, his conscience will be clear, and he will have inner peace. Knowledge is power, it is said; but virtue is peace."

"If there is righteousness in the heart,
There will be beauty in character.
If there is beauty in character,
There will be harmony in the home.
When there is harmony in the home,
There will be order in the nation.
When there is order in the nation,
There will be peace in the world."

Love (Prema)

"I must tell you of the paramount importance of love. Love is God; live in love. God is the embodiment of perfect love. He can be known and realized, reached and won, only through love. You can see the moon only with the help of moonlight; you can see God only through the rays of love."

"The earth is a huge enterprise, a busy factory, where the product is love. By means of your spiritual practice, it is possible to produce love and export it to millions and millions of people in need of it. The more it is shared, the deeper it grows, the sweeter its taste, and the greater the joy. By means of love, one can approach God and stay in his presence, for God is love, and when one lives in love he is living in God."

Non-Violence (Ahimsa)

"Ahimsa (non-violence) does not mean merely not injuring a living being physically. You should not cause harm even by a word, a look, or a gesture. Tolerance, fortitude, equanimity – these help you to practice ahimsa steadily."

"Ahimsa is another facet of Sathya (Truth). When once you are aware of the kinship of all the beings, the fundamental inner unity and oneness with God, you will not knowingly cause pain or distress to another."

"If thugs attack you and chop off your hand, it is Himsa (violence). But, if the doctor amputates your hand in a surgery, he does it to save your life, and hence, it is Ahimsa (nonviolence). Non-Violence, therefore, is a matter of intention and attitude, directed from the heart."

The five truths are simple, yet human nature makes them difficult to follow. As Sai put it, "Human values are born with man. They are not got from outside. Man, in his ignorance, is not aware of these values. When man sheds his ignorance, he will experience his divine nature."

Shedding ignorance should most certainly be the goal of the healing centers, and that put the five values at the very center of our program. It was later, when we attempted to implement those five values, that I learned a very, valuable lesson about human nature.

Lesson: Learn To Live With Less

The goal of the centers, as I envisioned them, was to teach people how to live with less. It should be no surprise that such a goal is among the most difficult to attain in the Western world and other developing nations. After all, we gauge success on how much we have acquired. Our goal is bigger and better. Bigger houses, better cars, more cars, nicer clothing, expensive jewelry, plush hotels, swank restaurants; these are what we aspire to because more bling means greater success.

But the notion of living with less does not just deal with economic issues. It quickly turns into a spiritual issue when you ask the question, *How* do I live with less?

The answer: To live with less is to see everybody as equal.

This is another difficult concept to get your arms around. How can I be equal to the beggar in the street, you might ask, or the CEO in the corner office? How can I love mankind equally?

The answer to all of these questions comes down to the realization and acceptance that there is a piece of all of us, in all of us. The priest, the prostitute, the liar, the philanthropist, and so on, are contained in each of us. "Every person you see is a part of you", said Carl Jung, the father of analytical psychology, who went on to say that, "You

172

cannot identify something in humanity that is not in you. Everything that irritates us about others can lead to understanding of ourselves", said Jung.

Are you interested in understanding yourself and promoting a sense of equality with others? Try this three-part experiment:

1. Search yourself: Next time you see someone you don't like, dissect your feelings. Why don't I like this person? What are the specific elements about them that I don't like and would like to never see again? Think about them very carefully and write them all down.

2. Turn the tables: Do you have the elements of your disdain written down? Look at those elements and think about them as they relate to yourself. Are you sometimes judgmental, or have to fight feelings of being judgmental? How about self-centered like someone you outspokenly dislike? Do you want to be flirtatious like that person you dislike for being flirtatious? Do you have argumentative tendencies that you suppress and yet secretly admire them in a person you say you detest? There are thousands of elements that make up our personalities, and you have all of them, like it or not. Look at the negative elements you have written down and honestly explore the role they play in your psyche.

3. Remember your findings: The next time you look at somebody and think they are not a nice person, remember that the same element you don't like in them, exists in you. Think quietly and carefully what it is about them that you don't like and realize that it is also contained in you.

Repeat this simple exercise several times; if you want it to be, it will become a habit. And then, mankind will become equal and your want will go away.

Questions & Answers

Question: How can living with less equal living with more?

Answer: When you live with less you realize that you actually need less. Realizing that helps develop the ability to share, which in turn makes you much happier. Chasing more catches you in the desire trap, and a desire cannot be fulfilled, ever, it just gets bigger and bigger.

Question: Has the meaning of the symbol given to you in a vision by Sai Baba totally revealed itself?

Answer: No. And, I don't expect it to. It is one of those symbols that has new meaning every time I see it.

Question: In relation to your wife Linda, you said, "We had literally freed ourselves from one another and in doing so were closer than ever." How does that work from a psychological point of view?

Answer: Instead of owning each other, or only loving each other if we supplied each other's needs, we allowed each other to be people in our own right. And so, we both became part of the whole. From a psychological point of view, it ceases you having to perform and allows you to just be. After all, it takes a lot of energy to keep performing, to keep up a pretense.

Question: Has being chosen to lead by a wise man changed the way you conduct yourself?

Answer: At first it did, because I thought I had to do or act in a certain way. But now I realize I just have to be who I am, and it is much easier. And, it makes more sense. I was chosen because of who I am, not chosen to then become someone else.

CHAPTER 8

Decoding Messages

"Anyone who wants to know the human
psyche will learn next to nothing from
experimental psychology. He would be better
advised to abandon exact science, put away
his scholar's gown, bid farewell to his study,
and wander with human heart throughout the
world. " Carl Jung

77 healing centers. Ways to show people how to desire less. Teach them how to meditate properly so they can live and eat consciously.

I got to work.

I told all of those around me about the centers. I told them about the mysterious task that had been given to me by Sai, and the apocalyptic date of 2020 that he gave me through someone else's dream. One thing I was learning fast, when I had a doubt about the experiences I was having, I'd always get confirmation through an event or person. "Divine backup" I call it, like Thomas in the Bible who needed to put his finger into Jesus' wounds to believe. I was getting much better at believing but must have needed this Divine boost. All I know is that Sai said, "The world's economy and food supply will somehow shift, and mankind will be better off if we desire less."

I had to admit that I didn't know what I was doing or why. Beyond the cryptic message from Sai Baba that I should create 77 healing centers, I had not received any particulars. I didn't know how big the centers were supposed to be, nor what was supposed to go on inside of them. I just knew they were healing centers, and (I thought) that Sai Baba wanted me to build them. I was waiting for information, but in the meantime, I had decided to move forward with the mystery project.

I thought this lack of direction would keep people from getting involved in the project, but that was not the case. Volunteers came in droves to start centers. Hearing that Sai Baba saw an apocalypse on the horizon was all they needed to hear. Details could come later. The centers had to be started.

Before I knew it, over a dozen centers sprang up. There were centers that occupied living rooms, a large warehouse space, one woman even built a center in a spare bedroom. Since no one knew what was supposed to be done in these centers, they followed the Sai model of creating a space for meditation and prayer. And with these centers came more people who were interested in personal enlightenment, and in comprehending how it was that we are all linked one to another around the world.

More and more I understood how it was that Sai Baba worked. I had spent a considerable amount of time being angry about not having more contact with the guru. Then he gave me (I thought) an assignment to build 77 healing centers but was not specific as to exactly what that meant. Then more information about the healing centers came to me through a stranger who had a dream that contained information that she said was to be conveyed to me. And then I was to respond to this information, hoping that more information would be imparted before I made a mistake following the sketchy earlier information. It was like working on a puzzle without having all of the pieces. I had to maintain faith that the other pieces would somehow be delivered, while figuring out where the pieces I had belonged in the big picture. And, I had to have faith that the other pieces would come before I was ready to give up.

Working this way required a lot of faith, an attribute I still wasn't sure I had in sufficient quantity. When I tried to explain my feelings about my faith to Linda, I fell back on my Catholic upbringing and equated myself with the disciple Peter. Despite having witnessed many of the miracles of Jesus, including his transfiguration, and even walking on water himself, Peter doubted Jesus three times just to save his own life. Yet in the end, Jesus chose Peter to build his church.

"Peter was picked for his weakness, not his strength," I said to Linda.

"Yes, he was," she said. "He had to be convinced to be faithful because just seeing the truth wasn't enough for him, he had to have more."

In essence Linda was saying that I didn't trust my feelings. I knew that was true. I had to have something more solid than intuition, and I set out to find it.

Leaving my family and practice once again, I returned to India, hoping to just observe Sai and his organization. With now 13 healing centers to oversee, I was having organizational problems that needed to be dealt with. Human nature had taken hold, and some of the people running the centers had gone rogue. Some were not teaching the five values – love, truth, peace, non-violence, and right conduct – and a few were not living them. Others had completely left the road to consciousness and had turned their centers into moneymaking ventures, complete with dues for belonging to their "meditation clubs". Not that making money is bad, it is just important how you spend that money. It was more a loan, really, that you should pay back with interest to help all of humanity, not just yourself. A lesson in greed versus need.

This had all taken place in a period of about a year, and with more people interested in starting new centers, I had come to realize that I needed organizational help to keep the venture from turning into a nightmare.

Also, I had been designing a healing center of my own with an architect. I wanted to take the architectural plans to Puttaparthi where I hoped to have them examined by someone within Sai's organization; to make certain they fit the mold of what I thought Sai would want in a healing center.

And those were the reasons I returned to India time and again.

Puttaparthi has no lack of architects. There are hundreds of buildings in the ashram and around it, everything from the tiniest abode to hospitals and universities named for Sai Baba. It was my hope to corner several of these architects to see if the plans for my healing center in Dublin were all that would be expected by the swami.

Then someone in the room where I was quartered offered a suggestion.

"Why don't you take it to Darshan tomorrow and see if Sai himself will examine the blueprints," he said. "You don't know unless you try."

I agreed, and the next morning found me kneeling next to the long path of carpet that Sai would walk on to greet the worshipers. I had lucked out and drawn a number that gave me this coveted position; and now I held my rolled-up blueprints and was waiting expectantly for Sai himself.

The healing center was located on land next to our house. It could hold a maximum of 30 devotees and contained the offices for my practice, which had thrived beyond my wildest dreams after my involvement with Sai Baba. If I could get Sai to look at the blueprints for a few moments, I knew he would be thrilled with its clean lines and wooden floor, and could tell me if I had missed anything and if so, how to fix it.

Sai Baba was coming down the carpet now and I held the blueprints up in anticipation of him unrolling them and giving me a moment or two of consultation.

That didn't happen.

The guru passed by the blueprints and my smiling face as though he hadn't seen either one of them, as though they didn't exist. I was disappointed to see his back to me, walking away down a hedgerow of hands, all reaching to touch him, or give him a note, or a token, as he strolled down the red carpet. At the height of my disappointment he turned and came back. In a moment he was standing over me.

"Put me on the toilet wall, will you?" he said, pointing to the blueprints. Then he walked away again.

I didn't have a clue as to what he meant. Put me on the toilet wall...what did he mean? I looked at the people around me, all of whom had blank looks on their faces. One of the men shook his head. "It must be us that don't understand. Sai Baba doesn't make mistakes!"

Another in the group said he was an architect, and suggested we go outside and roll out the blueprints to take a look. Another said he had no idea how Sai could make any determination at all without seeing the actual blueprints first. "I think he was joking," he said.

We all made our way out of the hall and into the bright sunlight where we spread the blueprints out on a concrete table. There we all hunched over the drawings and began searching for the toilet. Suddenly one of the Puttaparthi veterans stood straight up.

"I know what the problem is," he said. "Sai's picture is on the toilet wall, which faces east; but if it isn't on that wall, the Puja room will be facing the wrong way."

When he said that, we all began nodding. The Puja room is a small prayer room that contains the symbols of spirituality in every healing center. Sometimes it's a statue of Buddha, or a picture of Jesus; for us, the symbol was Sai Baba and it was hanging on the wrong wall. The wall of the toilet was where it was on the blueprint, which would have been facing in the wrong direction.

We all stood and looked at one another.

"He had never seen these blueprints, is that correct?" asked one of men who I judged to be a lawyer, given that he asked the question like he was conducting a deposition.

"Never," I said.

"And you never spoke to him about your healing center?" asked a woman.

"Never," I said.

"So, he didn't know in advance what the blueprints were for?" asked the man I assumed was a lawyer.

I froze for a moment.

"He obviously knew what kind of building the blueprints represented," I said. "He told us to change the wall his picture was on. He knows what the blueprints were for, but I don't know how because no one told him."

Everyone stood and looked at one another. Then we bent over the blueprints so I could change the wall in the Puja where Sai's picture would be hung. With a sharpie marker I highlighted the correct wall for Sai's picture and then wrote in front of it, "Sai hung here."

In retrospect, I can say we were all amazed that he was able to tell what the blueprints were for, and that his picture was hung on the wrong wall; but we weren't surprised. Very little Sai Baba did surprised any of the veterans of Puttaparthi.

A couple of days later I returned to Darshan, where I was lucky enough to draw a number that put me a row back from the carpet. I had my corrected blueprints with me, and when he walked by, I unrolled them so he could see the change in where his picture would be hung.

When he slowed down to take a look at the drawings, I said jokingly, "It's a good idea to have your picture on the toilet wall. That way you can flush the shit out of people."

He nodded at me and grinned like a man about to deliver revenge. Thirty seconds later, I felt urgency in my colon that couldn't be ignored. Breaking out in a cold sweat, I handed the blueprints to someone to hold and ran to the nearest toilet, a victim of severe diarrhea that was no doubt a gift of the swami himself.

***

Watching Sai Baba was some of the best psychological training I ever had, and this particular trip revealed some of Sai's best techniques. I called these techniques "Saicology" because no one could do them the way Sai could.

There were times when Sai ignored the faithful, driving them to search inside themselves for answers without him saying a word. One of those times was when he stopped showing up for Darshan for no apparent reason. It just happened one day. Thousands of people arrived at the stadium where they expected to see Sai and instead, they got nobody. The next day the same thing happened; Sai didn't show up.

The faithful became worried. They thought he was ill and unable to come out of his quarters. That isn't right, said some of his house workers. Sai isn't sick. Sai says there is an issue within the community, and we need to discover what it is and figure it out before he will return to public view.

This went on for eight days until some of those close to Sai hinted that the cab drivers were overcharging westerners and middle class Indians for their services. Sai, it turns out, felt the drivers were gouging worshipers, and decided to stop their source of income until they normalized their fees.

The beauty of this method was that it forced self-examination among all of the worshippers, who immediately began to examine their way of life and how their actions might be negatively affecting the mental state of their swami. If there was something that upset Sai, it was said, then we should all be aware of it because it was something that would eventually affect us all.

Another example of Sai-cology, came during interview time, those rare moments when about 30 people were allowed to crowd into a tiny room and ask the guru questions. It was times like these that his psychic abilities truly shone.

I was present during one interview session when an arrogant priest was confronting Sai, asking him if he truly thought he had the powers of a Jesus, or if he was just pretending to have them. The priest was acting very rude and Sai was trying to ignore him by answering questions from those on the other side of the room. Finally, in the midst of a rude outburst, Sai turned facing the priest and said, "Your problem is too much bad thoughts about sex!"

The priest froze for a moment and then began weeping. He admitted that he had been having an affair with one of his parishioners and was afraid that her husband was going to find out and report him to the bishop.

"I can't leave her," the priest moaned. "I know it's unholy, but it is something I have never experienced before."

The room became very uncomfortable as the priest sobbed softly. He told us all that he was thinking of leaving the priesthood, the thought of which was breaking his heart. Sai just sat patiently – a slight smile on his face – and listened.

"No, no, no, no, no, I am not talking about you, Father! I am talking to the young man in front of you. His problem is too much sex thoughts!"

When people ask what I mean by "Sai-cology," I define it as psychological techniques through which people will reveal themselves. As Sai so eloquently stated, "All spiritual practice must be dedicated to the removal of the husk and the revelation of the kernel."

Much in the way that Sai interacted with people I have been able to use in my own life and practice. But there are things he did that I have only been able to observe. In the beginning this bothered me. But over the years I have come to realize that if there was anything I needed to know, it will come to me, sometimes in mysterious ways and, at other times, in very direct ways that come like bolts from the blue.

One of those bolts from the blue hit me on this trip when I was in Puttaparthi. I was in a tiny room filled with landline telephones, which was the only way we could

communicate with people back home from India. My
world had expanded greatly. In addition to my psychotherapy practice, which had grown beyond my wildest
dreams, I had 13 healing centers to oversee and those
were becoming somewhat of a nightmare.

I was faced with constant questions about goals,
techniques, purpose, even janitorial advice. And those
were the easy issues to deal with. Other problems involved
greed and power. Some of those who had started centers
were now trying to charge membership fees instead of asking for donations, which is the standard way of garnering
support. And then there were the larger problems, ones
in which the founders of some of the centers had glorified
views of their role and began to think that they, and not God,
should be the object of veneration. All of these problems
had combined into a nightmare for me. I wondered how it
was that I would direct 77 centers without turning into an
average bureaucrat.

As I sat in the telephone room making calls, I became
aware of a man who was seated behind me. He had completed a telephone call of his own and now he was just
sitting behind me, listening. I found his presence annoying. It's bad enough when someone eavesdrops on your
conversation, but it is particularly bad when every person
you speak to on the phone has a complaint that they expect you to solve and a stranger is listening.

After listening to what must have been my tenth call, the
man spoke up.

"I can't help but listen to your conversations," said the
man, who had the confident air of someone who had spent

considerable time at the ashram, and wasn't shy about in-terjecting himself into another devotee's business. "You are talking to people who have started centers?"

"Yes," I said. "I have helped start 13 centers so far. At the swami's suggestion, I will start 77, although it's becoming very difficult and I don't know how I can bring myself to do that."

"77?" the man asked. "Why 77?"

I told him the whole story, how Sai Baba had appeared to me during a group meditation and drew a symbol on my spine. I told him how I had drawn that symbol on a piece of paper and taken it to a Darshan where Sai had stopped and asked for it, even though I had concealed it up my sleeve.

"This symbol will help you build your 77 healing centers, is what he said to me," I told the mysterious man. "He said when the world's economy collapses, he will fill my 77 centers with lost souls."

The man nodded his head sympathetically.

"Did he tell you how to build the 77 centers?" he asked.

"No, that's the problem," I said. "I tried to ask him, but he walked away. I can still see him walking down the carpet and looking back with a smile. But he ignored my questions. How do I build a center and what is a center anyway?"

The man scooted his chair closer.

"I have bad news and good news," he said. "Which do you want first?"

"The bad news."

"Okay, the bad news is that he was not talking about the centers in a literal sense," said the man. "So, you have wasted your time and the time of others by starting these centers."

"And the good news?"

"You don't have to create 77 centers," he said. "You can tell everyone that you misunderstood Sai Baba. He was not talking about creating 77 centers, he was talking about perfecting your centers."

That was the moment I discovered that Sai Baba had a plan for me.

***

"Frankly, nobody could put together and manage 77 healing centers," said the man, whose name was David. "For one thing there is no information as to what a healing center is. For another, no one person can be expected to oversee such a disparate spiritual empire. Too many people, too many personalities, too many different goals, no cohesion, too much power, too much ego...."

We were sitting at an outdoor café now, and David was analyzing my situation. He knew how Sai Baba worked. He had been coming to the ashram for 20 years and had heard many stories about people making bold assumptions based on small bits of information. Not to worry, he told me. Sai Baba works that way and with good reason.

"If he gives a devotee just a piece of information, that devotee will search for the remainder of the information," said David. "It becomes a learning experience for the person who goes down many blind alleys until they find the right path. It is frustrating, but effective. There are some very learned people here."

"So, what's the right path?" I asked.

"Here's what I think," said David. "According to yoga practice, we have 77 wheels of energy in our bodies: 7 major wheels and 70 minor ones."

"Where are they?"

"They are all over the body. But the seven major ones are: your crown, your third eye, throat chakra, heart chakra, solar plexus, your hara and your base chakra," said David. "Sai didn't tell you to create 77 healing centers, he told you to heal YOUR 77 centers, to create healing in them."

"Heal my centers?"

"Yes, heal your centers, fill them with light because they are supposed to be filled with energy and light," he said. He could see that I was confused by his answer. "You know, fill your healing centers with light and energy by proper meditation."

"And then what?"

"I don't know," said David. "Did he say anything else?"

"Not to me directly, but a woman came to my office and said that Sai spoke to her in a dream about what I was supposed to do," I said.

"And?"

"He told her that I was supposed to heal my centers to help people adjust before the year 2020," I said. "My goal would be to get people to understand what is really going on in the world economy so we can all begin to adjust before 2020."

"Well that's it," said David. "Your goal is to be a big draw – a big life – one filled to capacity with light."

"What does that mean?"

"It means that the universe has big plans for you! Get ready!"

***

David represented one of the many things that were good at the ashram. Because we were all strangers in a strange land, we practiced open communication. It wasn't unusual to overhear a conversation and jump right in like you were a part of the conversation all along. That's how it was and is at Puttaparthi.

I appreciated David's input on the 77 centers, and after meditating on what he said I realized he was right. Sai did not mean for me to go out and start 77 healing centers. He did mean for me to heal my 77 centers, the healing pathways that cover all of our bodies, from head to toe.

He was also right in assuming that I was to take a leadership role in preparing myself, then others, for the year 2023. That was one thing I interpreted correctly, not only from what Sai Baba had told me, but from other messages I was getting.

People were flocking to my practice now. Some from word of mouth, others because, as one woman said, "I just felt you had something for me," and others still because they had psychic flashes or dreams that led them to my clinic. Of those, several said that by the age of 45 I would become a brilliant leader, a spiritual force that would guide people to enlightenment.

I began to have dreams myself that felt psychic in their content. In one, I was sitting by a river and I had a long beard and grey hair. I was sitting by a big rock with the sun bearing down, and I was feeling perfectly calm and cool, despite being in the middle of Madison Square Garden talking to thousands of people.

This dream was a coming reality, or so said many psychics, as well as people at the ashram. They knew this because Sai was treating me like "one of his chosen seeds," as someone at the ashram said. They noticed that Sai Baba looked my way at Darshan, that he smiled or locked eyes with me, or gave some kind of gesture that made it clear he was keeping a favorable eye on me.

I heard all of these accolades, I really did. But I was also sensing something else on the horizon that was grounding and substantially less pleasant. I had developed a cough, a serious hacking cough that persisted well beyond what seemed normal.

I have had many illnesses in the past that required me to take medication, yet because of my training, I always chose to do meditation to heal it out of my mind and body. That's because I had learned that everything is energy. I was able to check my own body for illness and using techniques like Pac-Man or Painters Pallet (these techniques are on my website). I would change the energy to wellness and balance, and the illness would disappear. I am not saying this is for everyone, I am saying it saved my life many times. And I did not have to deal with medication's side effects.

By examining the situation around my illness, I discovered a lot about ego that applied to other parts of my life. I discovered that the best way to make a decision, is to first be still. One can't make an important decision when emotions are rising. You have to allow the emotions to leave you before you can ask your higher self, or God, what it is you should do.

How does one do this? My method of self-examination is through meditation, particularly the one I have included in the lesson at the end of this chapter. There are many forms of meditation, but this one works best for me. As you begin to study, you might find that other forms of meditation are better for you. The search for the perfect form of meditation is part of the search you are on, the one that is your path in life.

Whatever form you eventually select, meditation will provide answers about who you are. You, also, have to understand that the answer you come up with – for your best and highest good – may not be what you expect. It may produce consequences that may be very challenging; although that path might be challenging, it is the way back to your true self.

In hopes of avoiding challenge, your ego may try to convince you that you will be a loser if you take that path, or that by avoiding your true path you may encounter suffering. Take that path anyway, especially if it leads to the person you truly are. Living within your true self is vastly preferable to living a lie.

I also realized that living within your true self creates a healthy ego, something that is important to all of us. Healthy ego is what gives us all self-respect. Unhealthy ego is what makes us think too highly or unrealistically of ourselves.

As the Bible puts it, "Pride goes before the fall," which is a perfect explanation for the balancing point between healthy and unhealthy ego.

I realized that thinking that I would be responsible for starting 77 healing centers was not logical, and revealed a flaw in my ego. Sai helped reveal that flaw by being vague about what the 77 healing centers meant. He meant that I should perfect the healing centers in my body, and that by doing that, I would become a spiritual leader, helping people through hard times. He did not mean that I should start 77 healing centers. It was my ego that had told me to do that, the type of ego that tells a person to push forward, without truly understanding what they are pushing, and where they are going or why.

I now realize that everything contained in this book, from believing I was chosen to create 77 healing centers, to the cancer that came and went, were given to me as lessons to improve the health of my ego.

Now that I understood the nature of my ego, things would be different. I set out to do what was intended; make myself ready for the hard times, when an enlightened form of myself would be needed.

Lesson: A Self-Examined Life

"The unexamined life is not worth living," said Socrates. From a man known for boldness, that is one of the boldest things he said. What this means to me is, that one must explore the motivations of how they react to life, namely, why do we do what we do? And most importantly, how can we do it better?

There are many ways in which one can examine their life. The choice for me is meditation, the act of thinking about something deeply, or (and this seems contradictory) the act of emptying your mind of all thoughts and thinking of nothing.

There are many ways to accomplish either the full or the empty forms of meditation. I will discuss different methods later on; but for me now, I am practicing Contemplative Meditation in which I merely walk through the city (I live in Dublin and Los Angeles) and contemplate all that is around me. I focus on the beautiful woman walking past me, the homeless man on the sidewalk, the coffee and doughnut sign in the Dunkin' Donuts shop, the Ferrari cruising slowly next to the city bus. In other words, I stay in the now by observing without judgment, all that passes and is around me. Sometimes these meditative walks are only for a mile or so, but there have been times when time gets away from me, and hours pass before I return to a non-meditative state…and I mean hours. I have had days when I have walked 5 or 6 hours unaware of the time.

Try it yourself. Dress in comfortable clothing and shoes and start walking. The meditation part comes with a change in attitude, in which you observe, but don't think deeply or judge. Actually doing this is more difficult, as you will find out once you try it. See that homeless man? Don't think either good thoughts or bad about him. Let what you see bounce off your conscious mind like a marble pinging off a concrete floor. Try not to focus too deeply on the external world, but keep your thoughts on your breath, breathing deeply and rhythmically as you walk. The order of the day is shallow thinking and deep breathing.

For me, contemplative meditation is merely a form of thoughtful observation. By being unaffected by the outer world, we are merging everything into one stream of consciousness with the eventual goal of feeling at one with the universe as it is, not as we judge that it should be.

CHAPTER 9

No One Ever Dies

"Every moment, everyone is nearing death.
Death is not a deplorable event. It is the
journey's end." Sathya Sai Baba

When I say that an interest in death was drummed into me, I mean that literally.

I woke up one morning in Puttaparthi to the intense sound of drumming. For several minutes I found it interesting and then it began to annoy me. The drumming was sharp and rhythmic and at times it sounded as though it was twenty feet away and getting closer.

I made my bed and dressed, and then went down to the cafeteria to have breakfast. The drumming was louder and more painful than it was from my room. That was apparently a sentiment shared by everyone else in the cafeteria because most had given up talking and were attempting to cover their ears and eat at the same time.

"What's with the drums?" I asked the man next to me.

"They're driving me crazy."

"Somebody's dying," he said. "When a loved one is close to death the family gathers and drum to keep the evil spirits away until the person dies."

I blushed and put my head down close to the bowl of oatmeal I was eating. I was embarrassed. Here I was complaining about a little noise, when somebody's loved one was about to transcend.

It's amazing how ignorant one can be of the world around them, I thought, finding meaning in this holy noise that didn't exist before.

Then, just as the drumming became a beautiful thing, it stopped. The lack of drumming left a void in the room that gradually filled with the conversation of others in the cafeteria. The man next to me tapped the table with his index finger. I looked up.

"The person died," he said.

A couple of hours later, on the edge of town, I saw a group of people carrying a body on a stretcher. It was wrapped in bright white sheets. Several men had the body hoisted to shoulder height and were followed by family and friends, many of whom played trumpets in a way that sounded to my Western ear like a disorganized New Orleans jazz band.

Whatever I had planned to do that afternoon, I cancelled it in favor of following the funeral procession.

They took a winding path down to the river, the body held high like a trophy or a sacrifice. At the river, the body was placed on a pile of wood. Words were spoken and then the man in charge of the business of disposing bodies lit the wood and it became a funeral pyre. Slowly the body melted, turned to bones and then to ash.

Later that afternoon I returned to the river and saw the family washing their clothing.

There was a beauty to the whole process for which I had no frame of reference. This is the difference between the Eastern view of life and that of the West, I thought.

It was then that I decided to practice the art of dying.

***

There are many ways to describe the art of dying. In most schools of Tibetan yoga there are six dimensions, each of which can be reached by different forms of meditation. It is a journey to pursue these various forms of meditation. Reaching each dimension requires a lot of "homework" on the part of the practitioner. These dimensions carry with them different levels of consciousness and clarity about life and death. If one becomes proficient enough at these meditations, they will be able to experience that bright clear light that we know exists in near-death experiences, when a person who almost dies reports seeing a bright light. This light may also cause a sensation, similar to orgasm, or the feeling one gets an instant before and after dreaming.

This moment is called a Bardo, meaning "the transitional state." There is the "Bardo of death," when one is transitioning to a dying state, the "Bardo of dreams," that moment before or after dreams, and the "Bardo of ordinary life" which you are in right now, the time between birth and death.

There are many elements important to the art of dying. One of them is the realization that each breath takes us closer to the finish line. Another element is that your last thought creates the karma for your next life. And still another element, you greet death not as an ending, but a "becoming," a beginning of time in another dimension.

No one ever dies, say Tibetans, we just keep recycling into another incarnation.

This was the reason a family could commit a loved one's ashes to a river in the morning and wash their clothing there in the afternoon. They don't believe in the death of consciousness, but rather that it returns to the flesh again and again, sometimes as a peasant and sometimes as a prince, and all the possibilities in between. They knew they weren't dead, just a consciousness ready for rebirth.

The thought that each breath takes us closer to our transition into our Bardo of death may not be a warm and comforting thought, but it certainly made me aware of how we spend our life and the breath that feeds our consciousness.

Linda agreed with that, and soon some of our meditation practice focused on the notion that life was practice for death.

I know this sounds negative, but it wasn't, not in the least. It was this kind of meditation, an art of dying approach, that made us aware of our own wealth and the amount of suffering in others we could contain by living with less. We began to provide financial support for many of the orphanages in and around Puttaparthi. By doing that we could literally see how a few dollars carefully spent made life tenable for children who would have had no hope otherwise. By meditating on death, we actually improved the lives of those around us.

Meditating on death improved our own relationship, too. We appreciated one another more than we had in the past. We had a greater focus on the finite aspect of life. This is something most people try to forget, but we found by focusing on our short time on earth, that our appreciation for one another grew as did our appreciation for the world. We soon made a pact that our service to the world was more important than our service to one another. We founded more orphanages and searched for other ways to build spiritual capital.

Life was good, largely because we were focused on death, our death.

Then it happened. As unexpectedly as rain on a clear day, Linda died.

Death Is An Illusion

There is absolute proof that death is an illusion and that we go on, helped on across by elders, family members, friends, masters, angels, and the Gods. This story is the story of a great being passing, my wife, Linda O'Neill.

The events began to unfold one day when I was in the healing center in Wexford. The phone rang, I picked it up, and it was my daughter, Orla, ringing to inform me that Linda had a severe headache, a sharp pain in her head, and she was feeling unwell – very unwell. Linda and I had not been to a doctor for many years, maybe twenty years or so, and I felt it very strange that my first response was, knowing of course that all can be healed through meditation or mind acts, my words, "Call a doctor". So, Gavin and Orla called a doctor, and when they described to the doctor the symptoms, the doctor says, "No, this is not a doctor case, you need to go straight to the hospital. I will send an ambulance." The ambulance took Linda to the hospital.

Upon her arrival in the hospital, after a period of waiting, Linda was seen by some doctors, and the diagnosis was that it was just stress, or a migraine of some sort. Linda was then told to go home for rest and not to worry; but over the next couple of days she began to deteriorate really badly. This deterioration led me to come up from Wexford to see how she was doing.

As I was there for a few days, I watched as Linda began to recover slightly and then deteriorate, recover slightly and then deteriorate, until one morning I was making her a cup of tea, and I asked her a question, and just for a moment she spoke with a lisp, or strangely disorientated kind of speech, and then I realized that the symptoms were that of a stroke. Knowing that Linda might begin to panic slightly about this event, I went to my daughter Orla and said, "Please go down and ask your Mum if you could bring her to a doctor, that you're worried about her, so that she would do it, because she would relieve the worrying of her daughter far quicker than she would relieve her own pain." That's the type of being she was.

Orla brought her to our GP, the family doctor of thirty years or so. It turned out that the doctor actually wasn't there when Orla brought her into the surgery, but another doctor was there, and strangely enough this doctor had once been in Sai Baba's super specialty hospital in Puttaparthi, India. Orla explained that whilst there, Linda had quite a severe reaction, and the doctor noted this and said she needed to go back to the hospital. He began to write a letter, in order for Orla to bring her to the hospital. Strange, of course, that the doctor never called an ambulance, which you imagine would have been the more appropriate response. As Orla was taking Linda, who was very weak at the time, out to the car, she was stopped and asked by the receptionist for the payment before she could leave, even though Linda was in quite a weak state and leaning on Orla. Orla paid and then went to the hospital, and on the way to the hospital rang me to inform me that Linda had taken another turn, and that she was on the way back to the hospital. I decided I would meet them at the hospital.

I arrived at the hospital, and to explain – the system in this hospital now was what's called a triage nurse system, which basically is a failure of the medical community, in that instead of seeing a doctor when you go to the hospital, you see a nurse. And then that nurse has to assess as to how serious the accident or event is, and then put you on a list of who would be seen first and last.

As I entered the triage nurse's room, she was stating that Linda was perfectly fine, because she was either just having a migraine, or the condition was stress-related as per the week before.

And I got quite annoyed and said, "Please, you need to understand that this is a stroke."

I mentioned the word "stroke" and the nurse said, "No, this is not a stroke because..." her coordination would be this, that or the other.

I said, "No, my father had taken a stroke, and his coordination was perfectly fine until it was too late; and in fact, also passed away from the same associated symptoms."

So I began to plead with the nurse to at least monitor her heart again or blood pressure, that this was a stroke, and just to appease me, she took Linda's blood pressure, which actually turned out to be extremely low at the time.

Then she said for us to wait outside, that a doctor would see us as soon as possible. This wait ended up taking something in the region of six to eight hours as Linda vomited, went in and out of consciousness, and became more and more weak. I had to go and attend to some important business, and by this time was convinced I was wrong, and they were right, and Linda would be fine. So, Orla stayed with Linda and kept me informed over the phone. Then when Linda was seen again by the doctor after six or eight hours, the doctors again agreed that it was only stress-related and nothing to worry about, and Linda was once again sent home for the second time.

This time when Linda was sent home, I wanted to keep my eye on her, but I also had my duties in the healing center in Wexford to attend to, so we brought Linda down to Wexford and looked after her there for several days. During those days she began to recover; I am absolutely sure, this had to do with the energy of the healing center in Wexford.

As Linda recovered, we brought her back up to Dublin, and while there the phone rang, and it was the nurse saying could we bring Linda in on Monday (this was a Friday) for tests, blood tests, etcetera, and I said to the nurse, "Please could we not bring her in now? I believe this is very serious, and in fact, she may not be with us by Monday," but the nurse insisted that we go in on Monday.

So, Orla once again brought Linda to the clinic on the Monday where they took blood tests. And then they took a CAT scan or an x-ray, and it showed some sort of a little disruption or patch, which caused them to begin to worry, and this worry then led to a doctor to say that it would be best for Linda to stay in the hospital for a day or two to undergo more tests. The problem was that there was no bed for her, so Linda ended up sleeping on a trolley with no pillow or anything for 24 hours whilst they tried to locate a bed for her. But things deteriorated a little further, and finally they ended up locating a bed for Linda on the second day, and she was admitted to the ward.

There they undertook more tests with Linda, and then she was generally just left in the bed for five days on aspirin tablets, and no other medication was administered during this time. We saw Linda in several different states of being during these days.

Then a sequence of occurrences began where Linda began to complain of chest pains and the like, and so we informed the staff of the hospital. And the doctor then had a monitor applied to Linda. This monitor was to monitor her for 24 hours to see if there were any irregularities.

After just several hours of this monitor being on, the nurse came to take the monitor off Linda. Orla said for it to be left on for the 24 hours, at which the nurse said that it was needed for another patient who was sick, more or less indicating, that Linda was some form of malingerer. This obviously caused great, great distress to my daughter, and then when they informed me, I also made note to the staff about this event.

The next big event was when Linda was to have a lumbar puncture, and the lumbar puncture was to happen at 11 o'clock, but in fact I arrived at the hospital at 8 o'clock on the Friday morning, and when I arrived Linda was lying very flat on her back looking very pale and weak. I asked her what had happened, and she said "Nothing, nothing happened, and nothing is wrong." I said to her, "Please, Linda, you and I can see that something is wrong. You need to tell us if something is going on." It was at this stage that she informed me that the lumbar puncture had not gone to plan, that in fact, there was great difficulty and instead of the procedure taking its normal period of time, it took much, much longer. I believe that this particular technique is extremely painful, and it should only take eight minutes, but it took something like twenty minutes in Linda's case, so she was in quite an uncomfortable state. So I sat with her that day, and then my son and daughter and daughter's boyfriend arrived at the hospital, and Linda motioned or gestured to me that I should go and look after whatever business I needed to look after, that she would be ok.

During the time that my son and daughter and daughter's boyfriend were at her bedside, a speech therapist came to assess her speech, and in fact, Linda's coherent speech was not good, i.e., when asked something like who was the president of America she said Bill Clinton, but it was in fact at that time, President Bush. When asked what her date of birth was, she took a long time to remember this type of thing.

She was getting stressed, and according to Orla and my son Gavin, she was getting more and more agitated. So much so, that when the test was over, she said to Gavin and Orla, what are now famous words in our family, "When this is over, there will be big changes." At this time, Orla and her boyfriend, Colin, went to get something to eat in the café downstairs.

Gavin stayed with Linda and was reading a magazine when Linda said to him, "I feel really tired but don't want to go to sleep."

Gavin said, "Don't be silly. Go to sleep, and I'll be here when you wake up."

Orla came back a while later to see how Linda was doing, but she was asleep by now, so Gavin and Orla went outside the room for a few minutes so as not to wake Linda. A while later Gavin went back into the room to see if she was still asleep, and while he was there the doctors came in to check on her. Gavin tried to wake her, but when she woke up, she was totally disorientated and could not speak or understand the doctors. At this time, the doctors asked everyone to leave the room. Orla then rang me and said, "Please, Dad, please, Dad, come, something is seriously wrong."

When I arrived at the hospital my sister and Linda's mother also had come to the hospital and were not allowed to see her. I said, "They won't stop me from seeing her," and I went in and went behind the curtains. The doctor asked who I was, and I said Linda's husband. The doctor then said, "Linda, your husband is here." Linda had no recognition of what he was saying. He then took a pen from his pocket and babbled with no coherent thoughts. The doctor then informed me that all would be fine, that there was no problem. It was just a little turn, and that they would bring her down now immediately for an MRI scan, to see what was going on in her brain in order to fix it.

I asked could we go down with her and was informed "No" – only one of us could, so it was deemed that I would go. We went down to the MRI section of the hospital. When there, the staff were not quite ready for her appearance, so Linda was just left outside the door and the nurse went to accommodate. I was holding Linda's hand, and her eyes were closed, and next she just opened her eyes, and at that moment, with great compassion, I saw that Linda was potentially about to leave this world. She squeezed my hand, and just at that moment the nurse arrived and wheeled her into the MRI.

I then rang Orla and Gavin who were upstairs and told them to come downstairs to sit outside and just support their mother while she was getting these tests, knowing full well, that something very dramatic was about to happen. That drama happened when all of a sudden, as we were sitting outside, we began to hear screams of Linda's name in a very frightened and fearful tone from the doctors and the nurses. Then a bit of panic started to set in, with the nurses and then with us, as Orla went into a complete and utter shock listening to the events unfolding. As I held her close in my arms, and comforted her, I realized what was happening.

Then the nurse came out and was in quite a state of shock, which was quite surprising because, as you know, nurses are sometimes quite used to these events. But, in some way, I'm sure Linda had touched them with her energy as she had many people during this event. The nurse was there with a tear in her eye saying that all would be ok, that the doctors were looking after Linda. Next, what looked like a crash team went in, and I believe Linda had a heart attack in the MRI machine. Then the doctor came out and said that there was no problem, that all was fine, that Linda had just vomited, or something in the machine, but because of the vomiting, some swelling had begun to occur in her head, and that she was now being transferred to the ICU unit.

As Linda was transferred, we all made our way up to the ICU unit. I began to ring all of Linda's family, her brothers and sisters, to come because I realized once again that this was the beginning of the end. When we had all gathered in the ICU, the doctor came, and he was in a great state of shock. He just kept saying that he didn't know what happened, he didn't know what went wrong Everything would be fine, he said, but there was some swelling and he was making arrangements to have Linda sent to a specialty hospital in Ireland for this type of stroke or injury. They would take Linda and reduce the swelling, and then she would come back to the hospital where they would then give her care. He was in quite a highly agitated, sorrowful state. I held his hand, looked him in the eye and said, "This has now gone out of your hands and has gone into a hand greater than that of yours or mine, i.e., the hand of God." But he kept insisting that all would be ok.

Then the ICU nurse came out and asked did we have a religion, and as I was about to say, "The religion of love," her sister said, "Yes, she's a Catholic."

The nurse then said, "You should send for a priest." It was at this stage that the whole family realized that Linda was in grave danger.

I said, "I am a priest, I am a minister; I will administer the Last Rites."

The nurse looked at me as if I had two heads because in Ireland ministers/priests aren't married and definitely don't have wives or children. So, I explained that I was a minister in an organization that allowed this. After a couple of moments, she said that it was ok to come in and carry out the Sacrament. I called Gavin and Orla to come in with me, but the nurse said that they couldn't come. This was beyond belief for me, so I just said, "They are coming," and put my hand across to block the nurse from preventing them from walking in. They came in and we all arrived at Linda's bed. She was wired and tubed up to every machine possible. At that moment I began to administer the Last Rites in a lineage that Linda and I had spoken of many times, called the Bardo Todal, which is the preparation for the leaving of the body in this life, to administer and get ready for your next life.

After this Linda was transferred to the specialty hospital, and the family and I followed. As we waited for Linda to be made comfortable, the doctor asked to speak to her husband and children. We were brought into a room and the doctor, who was an American woman, asked us what we knew about what was happening. So we explained that the doctor in the other hospital had said that she had got sick in the machine, that there was some swelling in her head, that the idea of sending her to this hospital was that you would relieve the pressure, and then she would be sent back to the original hospital and nurtured from there.

The doctor then became quite irate, nearly to the point of frustration or anger. And without thinking, said, "Are you kidding me? You must be joking. This woman will more than likely not make the night. And you should prepare yourself for this."

The shock of this once again for my daughter Orla was great, and I found myself holding Orla all night, trying to console her, as she just wept at the potential loss of her mother – not only her mother, her absolute best friend, and absolute support in this life. So, three days began to pass with all sorts of "maybe she'll make it, maybe she won't" scenarios that go on in these situations. During that time Orla could not sleep and stayed awake in the waiting room for the whole three days.

Then came the most relieving, or what we would now class as miraculous, event that gave us all peace of mind and heart. Gavin, my son, had noticed that there was no picture of Linda's spiritual teacher, Sathya Sai Baba, over her bed. He asked somebody, who was going home to get fresh clothes, to bring a special picture that he had in his bedroom. This person brought the picture and Gavin put it over Linda's bed.

Moments later, as Gavin was at the bedside on his own, an Indian doctor arrived into ICU, came to Linda's bed, picked up Linda's chart, looked at it, looked up at the picture of Sai Baba, and said to Gavin, "Do you know this man?" or "Who is this man?"

Gavin replied, "Oh, this is Sathya Sai Baba."

The doctor then asked, "How do you know this man?"

Gavin replied, "My mother and father and family are devotees of Sathya Sai Baba," and said that they had gone to him many times and received his Darshan, and that he was their guru.

So, the doctor then said, "Very happy, very happy." Then the doctor said, "I will examine your Mother." Taking out her stethoscope, she began to draw on Linda's body the symbol of the Prema Agni, which is the symbol associated with Divine Love that is also used as the logo for the charity work that we do; building schools and orphanages all over the world, but especially in India. Gavin watched this in sort of two minds. On one hand he realized what was going on, but on the other hand, he didn't have a clue.

Then the doctor said, "She will be fine, very good woman, very blessed woman to have been to this man Sai Baba," and that she would be fine. Then, taking up the chart, she said to Gavin something like, "Wrong medicine." Then she said, "I will be back in a moment, I am just going to check something," and walked round to the nurses' station to monitor all the machines.

After five or so minutes, Gavin was waiting and there was no sign of the Indian doctor returning. So, Gavin walked to the nurses' station. The doctor wasn't there, so he said to the nurses, "When will the Indian doctor be coming back?"

To which the nurses said, "What Indian doctor? There is no Indian doctor." And even if there were an Indian doctor, she wouldn't have been allowed to examine Linda because doctors have to have permission from the other doctors in order to examine their patients.

At this stage, Gavin had a realization that Linda had potentially received a visit from her guru, her teacher, Sathya Sai Baba, in a different form. As crazy as this all seems, these things happen all over the world all the time.

Coming out of the room, Gavin came into the waiting room and shared the story of what happened with Orla and me and one or two others. At this, Orla became very excited, very upbeat, and said, "I knew he would come. I knew he would come." She had written him a letter the day before, stating that if he came and looked after her mother that she would be a good person and dedicate her life to the service of others. This caused great relief and great joy.

And so that evening, we all had a good night's rest, Orla for the first time was able to sleep. I remained in a state of meditation rather than sleep. Then at 7 o'clock in the morning the nurse came into the room where I was and said, "Derek, I have some bad news. Linda had a very restless night. She had a severe heart attack and won't make it."

I thanked her for her work, and she looked at me with amazement, that I was taking this news with such grace and not anger or shock. I asked her if it was OK for us to go in and see Linda, and she said, "Sure." So, I woke Gavin and Orla gently and told them to get dressed.

When they came out I said, "Your mother had a heart attack and she will be passing away in a short time, if you would like to go in and talk to her." So, we rang once again all the family to come, because a lot of the family had returned to their homes.

And when we went in, Linda was lying there in a very glowing and yet weak state. I went to the nurse and requested that when she starts to go into her death, would it be possible to knock off the machine before we hear that beep that you hear when somebody has died, that I didn't want my children's last memory of their mother to be a beep. She agreed.

As Linda deteriorated and began to drop more and more into the lower and lower heartbeats, it was a very dull, dark, cloudy, miserable day in Dublin. Linda's bed was beside the window of the hospital and the curtains were open, but there was no light of any significance because it was such a dark, quiet, day. Then, at the moment of Linda's transition, the machine began to drop and gracefully the nurse's hand came around and just switched off the machine.

And as we stood there, the people who had made it to Linda's bedside, her sister, her daughter, her son, her daughter's boyfriend, the manager of Creacon, Jonathan, and I. I said to Orla, "Your mother will be passing. Now if you would like to put your hands over your mother's heart, she will say to you her last goodbye." I also asked Gavin if he wished to do this, so he did his own goodbye.

As Orla placed her hands over her mother's heart, the most amazing event unfolded. At this stage two nurses had come to the bedside, the one who had switched off the machine and another. Just at this moment a massive, clear light, the clearest light that I had ever experienced, broke from the clouds and began to descend in through the window, and the light narrowing from a wide light to a narrow light, rested on the back of Orla's hand, and going through her hand into Linda's heart chakra. At that stage, I saw many beings: Jesus, Buddha, Masters from all religions, angels, friends, and family coming from the light down to stand by Linda's bed.

I thought that I was the only one witnessing or seeing this. But as I looked around me, I began to realize that Linda's sister and everybody, even the nurses, were witnessing this event. As we all looked on in awe, I watched as Linda lifted from her body, was greeted by all these beings of light, and began to walk with them away from her body. At that moment Orla said, "I witnessed, I felt her last heartbeat," with joy and yet great sadness. Then, as quickly as the light came, it began to leave, but leaving in a quick and yet slow way. It lifted from the back of Orla's hand; you could nearly touch it, as it went to the window. From the window it began to go up, up, up into the clouds, and just before the clouds closed over once again, I could see Linda just turn and, with a great smile on her face, I heard her say, "Great changes are coming." The light disappeared. And we stood at her bedside in awe.

Believers and non-believers alike had just witnessed a great event, possibly one of the greatest events that we will ever be given to witness in this lifetime or any life-time...the death of a soul happily returning home to its creator to serve as a guide from the other side in the heavenly realms. To me, and now to Linda's sister, Orla's boyfriend, Orla, Gavin and Jonathan, our lives have been touched forever, and we knew, without a shadow of a doubt now, not to fear death, that death is just a happening, and that God is always with us, even if we deny God.

Hopefully, this story brings you some relief, that should you have to go through this event, or have already, that there is nothing to fear.

**

A few weeks after the death of Linda we met with the hospital staff, where our nightmare had begun. We had discussed every option from suing the hospital for neglect, to simply yelling at the doctors for their bad attitude and that of the staff. The attitude of an organization starts at the top, and no one is higher in a hospital than the doctors on staff. They should not have allowed the nurses to minimize or doubt Linda's pain, but that's what they were doing by diagnosing her with migraine headaches, without having any sound proof. She was not a complainer nor was she a hypochondriac, yet the doctors minimized her symptoms without exploring them further; despite the fact that she exhibited signs of a stroke from the moment she arrived at the hospital.

We discussed the possibility of suing the hospital, and were moving in that direction, when we started talking about an event that happened at Linda's graveside service. As we drove into the graveyard that day, a beautiful rainbow crossed the sky and went directly into the ground at the precise spot Linda was being buried. This site was beautiful to Westerners, but to those of us with Eastern spiritual beliefs it meant something more. In the Buddhist tradition, a high lama leaves their physical body and transcends through a rainbow. To our way of thinking, a rainbow that meets the deceased at their graveside would be of extra special meaning.

Just talking about the rainbow changed our thinking. Rather than going after the hospital aggressively, we decided to approach them with kindness. When we went into the conference room to meet the nervous group of doctors, we told them that we were not interested in suing them or the hospital, although we had considered it. Instead, we wanted to discuss ways to keep this from happening again to other patients.

The doctors were stunned. They expected us to be angry because they knew we had reason to be angry. Linda's complaints had been minimized and there was a good chance she would be alive now if they had acted responsibly. Yet the truth of the teachings say you will only die when it is your time, no matter what you do.

"Let's talk about ways this institution can change to make it safer and more user-friendly," I said.

Once the doctors got over being startled by our response, we had a long meeting, in which a number of possible guidelines were drawn up, including having respect for a patient's symptoms. After our meeting with the doctors, new guidelines were created to humanize the hospital, and have made a profound difference in the treatment of patients.

That was just one more thing Linda did for the world, and I wish she had been there to see it...or maybe she was.

Lessons: Lessons from Death

What happened to Linda has made me think hard about lessons I have learned from her death. There is one that sticks hard: Someday your life will flash before your eyes. Make sure it's worth watching again.

With that in mind, I have made a special effort to make sure I have a special life, one of caring for others while exploring the world for beauty and meaning. To do both of those, I keep four precepts in mind, ones you can most certainly implement in your own life:

1. Share your gift with the world. Art, masonry, medicine, bookkeeping.... We all have a gift that others need to know about. Share it with the world. If you are a good communicator, share your ability with others. If you journal or doodle, show others how to do it. When you share your gift with the world, you share a valuable part of yourself that lives on after you are gone.

2. Life is too short to be anything but happy. That is a sentence that explains itself but has even greater impact when you are attending to one who is dying. One of the many things that changed for me with the death of Linda, was that I focused on happiness. If you think about it, why would you do anything else?

3. Love everybody. Why do we not like some people? Is it because they are annoying? Is it because they don't agree with our politics? Do they talk too much? Are

they less fit than us? There are many reasons not to love someone, but most of them are not very good ones. Dislike of someone eats up a lot of energy, a lot more than love does. Love gives you more time for important things and puts your mind at ease. When people come to me and complain about others, I have two pieces of advice for them:

- Be of service to others and you will lose that place of hate inside you.
- Love as though there is no hate.

4. Now is the only time that matters. The past is written. The future is a dream. The only time that is truly reliable and relevant is the now. Right now!

CHAPTER 10

Finding Your Excellence

"Imagine that all of your doubts about your life
have melted away and have been replaced by
an ease and wisdom that is visible to all around
you. That is finding your own excellence."
- Derek O'Neill

I have come to realize that the past pushes us forward. It schools us by reminder. It punishes us. It pleasures us. It makes us smarter. It reveals our weaknesses.

The past is our teacher. Like the sleek nose of a jet airplane, we are always moving forward into the unknown future, pushed by the forces behind us. Happiness is the space between two sadness's, and sadness is the space between two happiness's.

And just what are those forces of the past made from? For me, they have been made of good and bad, love and hate, friends and enemies, joy and sadness, wonder, anger, amusement, frustration, courage, jealousy, pity. These and many other elements fuel my life. They fuel yours, too. They are the basic emotions, the elements that make up our past and push us into the future.

If I were to look at that list of emotions for the first time, I would be frightened, as perhaps you are. I would see a list of emotions of which many are negative. I would see moments of soaring happiness blotted out by periods of sadness, or moments of hatred or anger that make me feel shame to remember them. The first thing I would ask: Are these negative events pushing me in the wrong direction? The first answer I would give: Yes. The past in everyone's life has negative sides, events we wish didn't happen, because now they own us.

In yogic terms, these events block our energy or "healing" centers and affect the way we behave in the future. The belief that "past is prologue" is true if we allow it to be true. The question is: How do we keep the bad habits of our past from ruling our future? How do we keep them from blocking our positive energy? The answer? Find your excellence.

I had originally thought to call this final chapter "Finding Your Perfection," but I decided not to because finding perfection is completely impossible. Nobody finds perfection. Even the greatest of wise men have been stymied in their attempts to reach this godly state. There is even an argument to be made that perfection does not truly exist, that searching for it is like trying to find an end to infinity. Perfection is simply a definition for God, something that is without errors, flaws, or faults. So, I backed off from the word "perfection" and went to "excellence," which is quite different from perfection. In the framework of what we are going to discuss, excellence means finding your best and using it to keep pushing forward to greater excellence.

My focus in this, the final chapter, is to help you achieve excellence through self-knowledge. As Sai Baba said,

"Knowing your true self will help you work more effectively to reach your goals. It will lead you down the road to success. It will bring you a calmness that will improve your attitude and your relationship with others."

In short, self-knowledge is the way to discover yourself and find your excellence.

When I look back over this memoir, I realize that I have chosen to discuss those events in my life that led me to explore myself. Those events were both good and bad, but rather than let the bad ones take me down; I made an effort to learn from them. At first, I didn't quite know how to do that, but I tried anyway, bumbling around in my own way to find something that amounted to a positive handhold that would allow me to pull myself up. Later I found Sai Baba (or did he find me?), who taught me how to search for self-knowledge. In his indirect way, he showed me how to find my excellence with techniques that "remove the husk" of our defenses, and let us "examine the kernel" of who we are.

The kernels of who we are can be found in those 77 major and minor junctions that make up our meridian system, those lines of force that relate to various emotions in our lives. Emotional traumas in our lives can block these energy centers and can make us act in ways that are not conscious but are more like an unwanted reflex.

I'll give you an example, as it relates to anger and India, where a short line to the cafeteria consists of 500 people. There were many times at the ashram in Puttaparthi where someone would cut into the front of the line and fights would break out. It was always amazing to me to be in line at a spiritual community and see someone being dragged out by their hair because they cut in line. Isn't there a better way for both the cutter and cuttee to handle this? Still, even though these events took place at a spiritual community, it was an excellent way to see emotional triggers in action and witness firsthand why most of these people had come to Puttaparthi in the first place.

Of course, the eventual goal of all these people wasn't to learn how to fight their way to the front of the line. Their goal, like mine, was to become our own guru. That too, was the goal of Sai Baba, who counseled us to find self-knowledge and declared, "Have faith in yourself, your own capacity to adhere to a strict timetable of spiritual discipline."

In the pages to follow, I have included seven ways to become one's own guru. These are methods I have learned from my own life or from others who have struggled to reach personal enlightenment. These methods have worked for me, but I offer a caveat, in that they aren't the only way to enlightenment. Rather, there are many ways to lessen or stop the struggle. These are merely here to provide some guidance to your own long journey. Success and namasté.

Becoming Your Own Guru

1. Explore Your Emotions (Become Conscious)

When I realized that the 77 healing centers Sai Baba wanted me to prepare were inside me and not something I was supposed to create, I studied the body's meridians, to find the bad emotions that had clogged mine. In general, I realized that I was holding on to emotions that I should have let go. I also realized that if I didn't let go of these negative past events, they would rule my future.

Anger is a good example. Like many people, I had a hair trigger about some things, one being unaware drivers. If someone cut me off in traffic, I became angry. But when I started thinking about this source of anger – truly became conscious of it – I realized it came from something other than being cut off in traffic, it came from events in my early life.

The next time I was cut off, I didn't react. Rather I explored the roots of my feelings, searching for the reasons I was reacting so hotly. What does being cut off in traffic remind me of? I asked myself. It didn't take much time to realize that it reminded me of times when I was abused as a child, or when I was not given respect by my mother or father. In many ways I felt as though I was being ignored by other drivers, just as I was ignored when I was a child.

Once I became aware of the roots of much of my anger, I decided to work on awareness of my other negative emotions. I won't go into detail on what those were, but instead the solution. When I felt a jolt of emotions that indicated I was becoming angry or sad, anxious or dismissive, or some other negative emotional response, I stopped what I was doing, closed my eyes and took a deep breath. Then for a few seconds I retreated into my mind and explored the true root cause of my reaction. There I found a trigger that related to someplace or something in my past. It was like psychological archaeology, and I became very adept at digging through the layers of my life to discover the events that formed my psychological make up.

And when I discovered those events? I changed or re-framed them by reacting differently. My anger became humor, sadness was mollified by looking beyond a per-sonal slight or a short-term problem, anxiety became a problem that could be cleared up by bringing reality into a situation and holding fear back. Gradually I was able to see that my emotional response was often an irratio-nal emotional response, and by taking a few seconds to meditate I could remove the "ir" from irrational. When that happened, I realized that I had caused much of the struggle in my life and because of that I could eliminate it, too. With that realization, my healing centers became clear and a vast emotional change came over me.

2. Accept the Past

We are the past, but that doesn't mean it has to be our future. If we are mean, or greedy or angry, or some oth-er character trait that we consider unacceptable, the only true way to make a change in our future, is to accept these traits. It is by accepting what you were in the past that you can change your future you.

Let me give you an example. One of my patients was a rude and angry man whose presence infected everyone around him with fear and loathing. When he became my patient, he was in his late forties and wanted very much to change. His wife had left him, and his sons were no longer children and realized that their father was simply a miserable person. This man was alone and was realizing his emotional failings as a father and a human being.

Yet realizing his failings wasn't enough. He was trying to change but felt as though people were reacting to the "old" him, not the "new" him he wanted to be. The reaction people had to him made him angry. He felt he had changed, and couldn't accept that he was the only one who knew about that change. It became worse when his ex-wife pointed out things he had done in their marriage that weren't nice. When she talked about the past it was never with good feelings, and that always made him angry.

"Why can't they see the change in me?" he asked. "Because it's not there," I said. "You haven't accepted the past, so the past won't go away."

I explained to him that until he could truly own the mistakes of the past, he could not progress.

"The past cannot change," I told him. "But by accepting it, admitting to yourself and others that you had been on a wrong path and want to change, you can change. The past pushes you into the future, and by accepting it, your future becomes more excellent."

We are all products of our past, but we don't have to be prisoners of it. All that is required to step out of that prison is an acknowledgment that we are in a prison of our own devise. And then we are out, a new person, one who can use memory to make a clean new future.

3. And While You're At It, Accept the Present

We have little control over events surrounding our lives. No matter how much we think we have control, unexpected events happen around us every day. Sometimes these events are unpleasant. Automobile accidents, lost jobs, illness, divorce – the list of unexpected events that can plague us goes on and on. With each passing minute of each passing day, we can be taken down a path that changes our lives in an instant. That is the true power of now.

Our true power lies not in control of the world around us, but in the emotional control we use when we react to it. Are we reacting to events blindly by letting our emotions control the moment? Or do we have control over our emotions?

Let me give you an example from my own practice. A patient of mine returned home from a night on the town to find that his home had been broken into and ransacked. Of course, the scene shocked him, and he said that for a moment he had that sickening, disempowered, fearful anger that an intruder had violated his world. Then he decided to put acceptance to work. He redirected his energy into calmness and acceptance, telling himself that he was lucky not to be in the house when the possibly violent intruder broke in. He took an inventory of his emotions, and made a clear choice to take a positive view of the break-in by expressing gratitude that nothing had taken place, except damage to material goods.

This attitude is called a resourceful state, which is the ability to handle a difficult situation or unusual problem with emotional intelligence. It represents true acceptance of the now. An unresourceful state for this patient would have been to expend his energy expressing anger and victimhood.

Choosing the resourceful path requires one important change: thought before reaction. Most of our reactions to events in the world around us are reflexive. Anger after being in a fender bender is typical of the reflex reaction I am talking about. Such a reaction would be unresourceful. Thinking before reacting might lead one to be thankful the accident wasn't worse, or express gladness that they didn't find themselves in a wheelchair. That kind of thinking would be considered resourceful.

One more thing: people who practice acceptance tend to become much happier with themselves, largely because they come to realize that they are what they are and make the best of it. Within a short amount of time, their acceptance of themselves turns to self-love.

4. Change Something

Bad relationships, bad jobs, bad attitudes, they happen easily and "un" happen with great difficultly. These along with a number of other problems are called "ruts," and if you think you are caught in a rut, you probably are.

Some people define a rut as a form of insanity, as did Albert Einstein who declared, "The definition of insanity is doing the same thing over and over again and expecting different results." That pretty much defines what a rut is and what it does to some people as well. A rut is depressing and comfortable at the same time, because it represents a condition that we have settled for, a place where things don't get worse, but they don't get appreciably better, either.

So how are we supposed to break out of a rut? Answer: Have the courage to make a change.

I know, easy for you to say, Derek. But, it's also easy to do. If you can't make a big change – like leaving a bad relationship or a bad job – make some small changes. For example, if arguments with your significant other follow the same pattern, then figure out a way to break that pattern. Sometimes that might mean going into a room alone for 30 minutes and meditating until the subject of the argument dissipates, or perhaps taking a walk until the subject behind the argument becomes insignificant. Sometimes it might even mean that you swallow your pride and tone yourself down, knowing that it takes two to tango. If the gentle changes don't work, then it might mean it's time for more significant ones. The point is that one needs to make small and incremental changes first, to see if that moves us out of our rut.

5. Be Conscious, Stay Conscious

We have been programmed to fear things that are not there and ignore things that are. A car wreck makes for a dramatic story on television, one that fills us with fear, but it masks untold and important stories that should be the focus of mass media, things like mass starvation and gun violence.

Much of the world has become focused on acute problems over which we have little control, and ignore chronic problems like starvation, overpopulation, and wars.

I think mass media and advertising has people focused on petty problems, many of them insignificant ones, that detract us from the greater and more significant world.

I have no intention of delivering a political commentary here, at least not more than I already have. I think we all know how much of our, very powerful personal focus, is wasted on celebrity watching or gossip. But if you decide to examine your life and see that you are devoting too much attention to acute issues, and diverting your powerful personal focus from chronic issues, if you feel sorry for the New Jersey Housewives because one of them is having their Mercedes repossessed, yet coverage of the slaughter in Syria bores you, then you might wonder, how do I overcome this imbalance in empathy that is infecting my life?

The answer? Be conscious, stay conscious. Treat your mental diet as you would your physical diet, making certain that the acute (alarmist) information you take in doesn't outweigh the important information, that which truly makes you think and react in a thoughtful way.

To do this, spend a few days analyzing what it is you watch on television, or even more now on social media channels like Facebook, Twitter, etc., as social media channels are even worse than television. It is not all bad, but most would agree there is a lot of crap on there. I mention television because it is such a pervasive and powerful conveyor of information, that it is both a thoughtful and thoughtless medium at the same time. Does what you watch fill you with needless fear? Does it "shut off" your brain with worthless information? Or does it make you think positive thoughts or fill you with valuable knowledge? Being aware of what is going into our brain, is as important as thinking about the food we eat. And remember, just because an advertisement says you need a product, doesn't mean you really need it. White teeth, a snappier potato chip, or a sleeker car can't replace the glow of a person who truly lives a conscious life.

6. All You Need Is Love

Finally, personal transformation all comes down to love and empathy, particularly, unconditional love. Without it, your search for self will never be satisfied.

I know what you're thinking, Well, maybe that's true, but there are people I could never love, let alone forgive.

Actually, it is not impossible. Love is not only spontaneous, it can be learned. It is a trainable experience that we can self-generate if we are willing to put in the effort. Why should we put in the effort? Because love and empathy – the ability to understand another's feelings and even forgive them their trespasses – are the most important steps in self-discovery. So much so, that a wise man said, "The inability to forgive is like taking poison and expecting the other person to die."

How can we feel love for those who have betrayed us? After all, these feelings and painful memories are real, aren't they? Doesn't this alone make it right to hold on to the pain and anger we feel? Why should we replace these long-held feelings with anything less than disdain? And indeed, how can it happen?

I believe that meditation, even short spurts of it, is an effective way of building empathy or love for others. There is a considerable amount of medical research to back up this opinion. One study by Stanford University researcher Emma Seppalla showed, that practicing a "loving kindness" meditation for as little as seven minutes a day, promotes "a sense of social connection" that provides the person meditating with a higher sense of self-esteem, lower levels of depression, and a greater sense of love for one's fellow man. That is quite a payoff for a short daily meditation that calls for you to focus on love and kindness, and sets free the other feelings you might have. Soon, your feelings toward others will change, and your love even toward others who have wronged you, will deepen.

Such a love-based meditation will help you love others, and it will help you love yourself, too.

"Love is your life, your friend, your relative, your food and your everything," said Sai Baba. "If you do not love other human beings, that means you do not love God."

That is the message I want to leave with you. Except, oh yes...

7. Be of Service to Others

Feed the homeless... contribute to orphanages... become a role model for underprivileged children... assist at a hospice... buy a poor family's groceries. The list of possible service to others goes on and on. Find something you can do for others and do it. Give, in proportion, to what you receive.

In giving, you will find the peace, power, and self-understanding you've been looking for. By serving others, you serve yourself, because we are all connected.

Love Love Love,

Derek

ABOUT THE AUTHOR

Fondly referred to as the Celtic Sage, Irish-born spiritual teacher Derek O'Neill inspires and uplifts people from all walks of life, offering guidance to influential world leaders, businesses, celebrities, athletes and everyday people alike. Distilled from his life work in psychotherapy, a martial arts career and study with wise yogis and Indian and Tibetan masters, Derek translates ancient wisdom into modern day teachings to address the biggest challenges facing humanity today.

For more than 30 years, Derek O'Neill has been transforming the lives of thousands of people around the world through workshops, consultations, speaking engagements, media, and tireless humanitarian work.

Drawing on years of training in martial arts, which earned him the level of Master Black Belt, coupled with his extraordinary intuitive abilities and expertise as a psychotherapist, Derek has pioneered a new psychology, transformational therapy. His signature process, aptly named "The Sword and the Brush," helps clients to seamlessly transmute their struggles into positive outcomes, using the sword to cut away old patterns and the brush to help paint the picture of the new life that they require.

Inspired by his worldly travels, Derek and his late wife Linda formed SQ Foundation, a not-for-profit organization focused on helping to solve global issues facing humanity today. In recognition of his service, Derek was honored with the highly prestigious Variety International Humanitarian Award, Arts for India Dayawati Modi Global Award, Irish Autism Action Man of the Year, and Hearts and Minds Pride of Eireann. Derek currently serves on the Board of Directors at Variety International.

Author of *More Truth Will Set You Free*, the *Get a Grip* series of pocket books, a cutting edge book on parenting titled *Calm Mama, Happy Baby*, and several children's books, Derek also hosted his own radio show, "The Way With Derek O'Neill," which enjoyed the most successful launch in VoiceAmerica's history, quickly garnering 100,000 listeners.

To learn more about Derek O'Neill, to attend his next workshops, to order books, download teachings, or to contact him, please visit his website: **derekoneill.com**

OTHER BOOKS

'Get a Grip' Books
Abundance: Starts Right Now
Addiction: What a Cover-Up!
Anger: Who Gives a Shite?
Anxiety: To Peace
Bullying: You Won't Beat Me
Confidence: Easy For You to Say
Consciousness: It's All Over You
Depression: What's that?
Desire: Never Fulfilled but Grows
Dreams: The Best Messengers
Excellence: You Never Lost It, You Forgot It
Fear: A Powerful Illusion
Forgiveness: So I Can Move On
Gratitude: Yes Please
Grief: Mind Boggling But Natural
Happiness: You Must Be Effin' Joking!
Love/Divorce: Soulmate or Cellmate?
Mindfulness: Out Of Or In Your Mind?
Relationships: Would You Want to Date You?
Stress: Is Stress Stressing You Out?
Suicide: Fast or Slow
Weight: What's Eating You?

Other Books
More Truth Will Set You Free
Calm Mama, Happy Baby

Children's Books
Water Drop Coloring Book
The Adventures of Lucinda in Love-Filled Fairyland

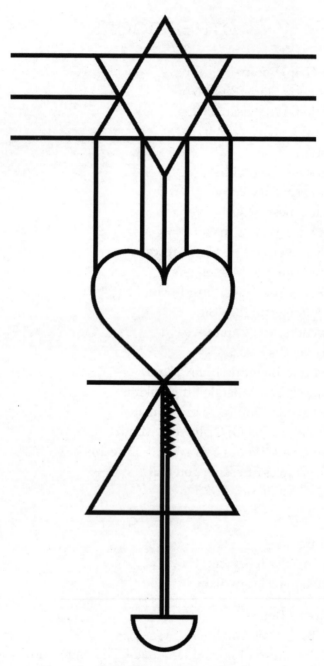

Aum Sri Premapranahuti